Open Learning Guide

Microsoft®
Publisher 2007
Introductory

Note:	*Microsoft is a registered trademark and Windows is a trademark of the Microsoft Corporation.*

Release OL323v1

Published by:

CiA Training Ltd
Business & Innovation Centre
Sunderland Enterprise Park
Sunderland SR5 2TH
United Kingdom

Tel: +44 (0)191 549 5002
Fax: +44 (0)191 549 9005

E-mail: info@ciatraining.co.uk
Web: www.ciatraining.co.uk

ISBN 13: 978-1-86005-542-3

Midland Books.
057-9321797.
(Edel.)

35

First published 2008

CiA Training's *Open Learning* guides are a collection of structured exercises building into a complete open learning package, to teach how to use a particular software application. They are designed to take the user through the features to enhance, fulfil and instil confidence in the product.

PUBLISHER INTRODUCTORY - The first guide in the *Publisher 2007* series contains exercises covering the following topics:

- Fundamentals
- Menus and Toolbars
- Task Panes
- Help
- Saving Publications
- Opening & Closing Publications
- Text Formatting

- Working with Text Boxes
- Tables
- Working with Pictures and Objects
- WordArt
- Using Pre-Defined Templates
- Creating Templates
- Using My Templates

This *Open Learning* guide is suitable for:

- Any individual wishing to learn *Publisher 2007* without any prior knowledge. The user works through the guide from start to finish.

- Tutor led groups as reinforcement material.

Aims and Objectives

To provide the necessary knowledge and techniques for the successful creation of publications using *Publisher 2007*.

After completing the guide the user will be able to:

- recognise the screen layout and use Help facilities

- save, open and close publications

- edit text and format text with effects, colour, bullets and numbering, etc.

- work with text boxes

- create and use tables

- insert and manipulate pictures and WordArt

- manipulate objects

- use the task pane to create publications easily

Downloading the Data Files

The data associated with these exercises must be downloaded from our website. Go to: **www.ciatraining.co.uk/data**. Follow the on screen instructions to download the appropriate data files.

By default, the data files will be downloaded to **Documents\CIA DATA FILES\Open Learning\Publisher 2007 Introductory Data**.

If you prefer, the data can be supplied on CD at an additional cost. Contact the Sales team at **info@ciatraining.co.uk**.

Introduction

This guide assumes that the program has been correctly and fully installed on your personal computer, that the computer is already switched on, and that a printer and mouse are attached. It may not be possible to access all of the **Clip Art** described without an Internet connection. The guide was created using version *2007* of *Publisher*.

Accompanying data for the exercises is supplied. This avoids unnecessary typing and speeds up the learning process.

Occasionally, long toolbars may be used and some of the buttons may be hidden. If this is the case, click on the chevrons at the right of the toolbar to reveal any hidden buttons. When using menus, double click on the menu title to display the full range of commands.

Notation Used Throughout This Pack

- Key presses are included within < >, e.g. **<Enter>**

- Menu selections are written, e.g. **File | Open** meaning select the **File** menu and then the **Open** command.

- The guide is split into individual exercises. Each exercise consists of a written explanation of the feature, followed by a stepped exercise. Read the ***Guidelines*** and then follow the ***Actions***, with reference to the ***Guidelines*** if necessary.

Recommendations

- It is suggested that users add their name, the date and exercise number after completing each exercise that requires a printed copy.

- Read the whole of each exercise before starting to work through it. This ensures the understanding of the topic and prevents unnecessary mistakes.

SECTION 1 FUNDAMENTALS..7

   1 - STARTING PUBLISHER 8
   2 - CREATING A BLANK PUBLICATION 9
   3 - THE PUBLISHER SCREEN 10
   4 - MENUS, TOOLBARS AND TASK PANE 11
   5 - HELP..13
   6 - TEXT BOXES 14
   7 - ZOOM 15
   8 - POSITIONING AND SIZING 16
   9 - CLOSING PUBLISHER..17
   10 - REVISION 18

SECTION 2 PUBLICATIONS..19

   11 - SAVING A PUBLICATION..20
   12 - CLOSING A PUBLICATION 22
   13 - OPENING A PUBLICATION 23
   14 - CURSOR MOVEMENT 25
   15 - SELECTING TEXT 26
   16 - EDITING TEXT 27
   17 - UNDO/REDO 28
   18 - DESIGN CHECKER 29
   19 - PAGE SETUP 30
   20 - PRINT OPTIONS 31
   21 - REVISION 32

SECTION 3 TEXT FORMATTING..33

   22 - CHANGING FONTS AND FONT SIZE..34
   23 - TEXT EFFECTS 35
   24 - DROP CAPS 36
   25 - CHANGING TEXT COLOUR..38
   26 - FORMAT PAINTER 39
   27 - ALIGNMENT 40
   28 - CHANGING SPACING 41
   29 - TABS 43
   30 - APPLYING BULLETS AND NUMBERING 45
   31 - SPELL CHECKING AND THESAURUS 47
   32 - REVISION 49

SECTION 4 WORKING WITH TEXT BOXES...50

   33 - TEXT BOX MARGINS..51
   34 - MOVING AND RESIZING TEXT BOXES 52
   35 - MARGINS AND LAYOUT GUIDES 53
   36 - APPLYING BORDERS AND SHADOW 55
   37 - FILLING TEXT BOXES..57
   38 - IMPORTING TEXT FILES...59
   39 - CONNECTING TEXT BOXES...60
   40 - COLUMNS...61
   41 - SIDEBARS AND CALLOUTS..62
   42 - THE SCRATCH AREA 64
   43 - REVISION 65

SECTION 5 TABLES...**66**

44 - INSERTING A TABLE 67

45 - ENTERING TEXT 68

46 - FORMATTING CELLS 69

47 - DELETING A TABLE 70

48 - CHANGE COLUMN WIDTH AND ROW HEIGHT 71

49 - INSERTING ROWS AND COLUMNS 72

50 - MERGING AND SPLITTING CELLS 73

51 - CREATING CELL DIAGONALS 74

52 - REVISION 76

SECTION 6 PICTURES **77**

53 - THE INSERT CLIP ART TASK PANE 78

54 - INSERTING AND DELETING PICTURES 80

55 - IMPORTING A PICTURE 81

56 - MOVING, RESIZING & CROPPING PICTURES 82

57 - ADDING BORDERS AND COLOUR 83

58- CREATING A WATERMARK EFFECT 84

59 - WRAPPING TEXT AROUND PICTURES 85

60 - REVISION 86

SECTION 7 WORDART **87**

61 - WORDART 88

62 - EDITING WORDART TEXT 89

63 - CHANGING WORDART SHAPE 90

64 - CHANGING LETTER HEIGHT AND SPACING 91

65 - ROTATING WORDART 92

66 - FLIP TEXT 93

67 - REVISION 94

SECTION 8 WORKING WITH OBJECTS **95**

68 - SELECTING MULTIPLE OBJECTS 96

69 - FLIP AND ROTATE OBJECTS 97

70 - CUT, COPY AND PASTE OBJECTS 98

71 - CUT, COPY AND PASTE TEXT 99

72 - LAYERING, ALIGNING & NUDGING OBJECTS 100

73 - DRAWING OBJECTS 102

74 - REVISION 104

SECTION 9 TEMPLATES **106**

75 - INTRODUCTION TO TEMPLATES 107

76 - SIGNS AND FLYERS 108

77 - CERTIFICATES 109

78 - GREETING CARDS 110

79 - CD/DVD LABELS 112

80 - CREATE A TEMPLATE 113

81 - USE A CREATED TEMPLATE 115

82 - REVISION 117

ANSWERS...**118**

GLOSSARY **123**

INDEX **125**

OTHER PRODUCTS FROM CIA TRAINING **127**

Section 1

Fundamentals

By the end of this Section you should be able to:

Start *Publisher*

Create a Blank Publication

Recognise the Publisher Screen

Use the Menus, Toolbars and Task Pane

Use Help

Use Text Boxes

Zoom In and Out of a Publication

Use Positioning and Sizing Guides

Close *Publisher*

Exercise 1 - Starting Publisher

Guidelines:

Publisher is a desktop publishing program, which helps create impressive publications easily. Each item within a publication, e.g. a picture or a text box, is known as an **object**.

Objects can be moved around and changed to create impressive effects. The methods used to move, resize or format each object are the same, so once they have been learned, complex publications can be created.

There are numerous ways to start *Publisher 2007* depending on how the computer has been set up. The following exercise describes the normal method for starting *Publisher*.

Actions:

1.   Click [icon] to show the list of **Start** options available. All *Windows* applications can be started from here.

2.   Move the mouse to **All Programs**, then click **Microsoft Office** and then move the mouse over **Microsoft Office Publisher 2007**.

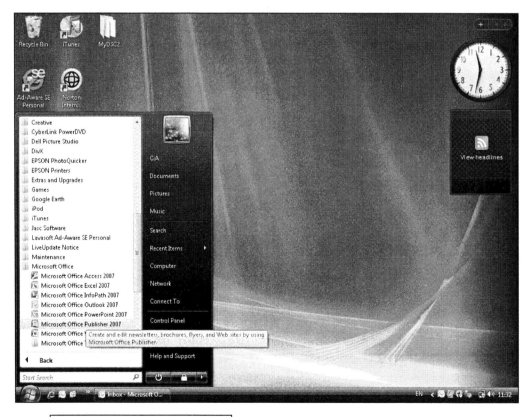

3.   Click [Microsoft Office Publisher 2007] to start the application.

Exercise 2 - Creating a Blank Publication

Guidelines:

The **Getting Started** window is *Publisher's* way of helping you create a publication – the universal name for the finished article. There are numerous templates available to use. A template is a ready-made publication that requires only the text to be edited or maybe a picture to be changed, resized, etc.

Actions:

1. Look at the **Getting Started** window. This is displayed when *Publisher* is started. If not, from the menu, select **File | New**.

2. Select **Blank Page Sizes** from the list at the left. This displays a list of the different types of blank publication available.

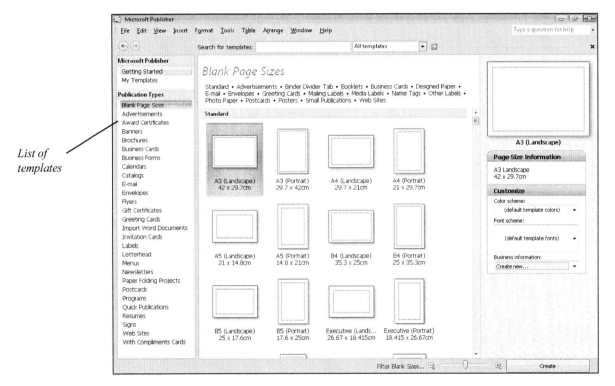

List of templates

3. A blank **A3 Landscape** page is selected by default. Click on the different pictures (thumbnails) of publications to see the other options.

4. Select **A4 Portrait** by clicking on it twice. The blank, single page publication is created, ready for editing.

Note: *If a prompt to save your work appears in these early exercises, select* **No**.

5. The **Format Publication** task pane is displayed at the left of the screen. Click the **Close** button, ☒, to remove it and allow more space to display the publication. From now on, it is assumed that you will close the task pane whenever it is not being used.

Exercise 3 - The Publisher Screen

Guidelines:

After a publication has been selected from **Blank Publications**, the *Publisher* screen appears, displaying the page to be edited.

Actions:

1. Notice the blue **Title Bar** at the top of the screen. This shows the name of the current publication (**Publication1**), the name of the application (**Microsoft Publisher**) and **Print Publication**.

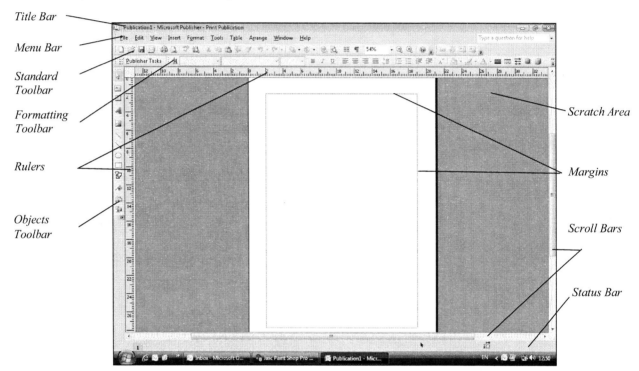

Title Bar

Menu Bar

Standard Toolbar

Formatting Toolbar

Rulers

Objects Toolbar

Scratch Area

Margins

Scroll Bars

Status Bar

2. Look below the **Title Bar** to see the **Menu Bar**. All of the commands necessary to use *Publisher* are contained within these menus. Below the **Menu Bar** are the **Standard** and **Formatting Toolbars**, made up of shortcut buttons (or tools) to perform common tasks more quickly.

3. Look at the buttons on the **Formatting Toolbar**. Many are ghosted (pale and not available for selection) because there is nothing on the page to be formatted. Notice that the **Objects Toolbar** has more active buttons available as these tools are used to create various objects on the page.

4. Notice the grey **Scratch Area** around the page, where objects can be dragged and manipulated before being placed on the page. At the bottom and right of the page are **Scroll Bars**, which allow movement up and down, or from left to right.

5. The **Status Bar** at the bottom of the screen shows the number of pages in the publication and the **Object Position** and **Size** areas. Move the cursor around the screen and its position relative to the top left corner of the page will always be displayed in the **Object Position** area.

Exercise 4 - Menus, Toolbars and Task Pane

Guidelines:

The **Menu Bar** contains all of the commands needed to use *Publisher*, within drop down lists. **Toolbars** allow quick access to the most commonly used commands and each command is represented by a button. To save space on the screen, the **Standard** and **Formatting** toolbars can be displayed on a single line. This means that many buttons are hidden, but they can easily be displayed.

The **task pane** can be used to help perform common tasks more quickly. It is often activated when a particular menu command is selected, but can be displayed at any time.

Actions:

1. Move the pointer over the word **Edit** and click with the left mouse button to open the **Edit** menu.

2. Notice how some of the commands are ghosted (pale). This means they are not available for selection at the moment.

3. Close the **Edit** menu by either clicking outside the menu or click on **Edit** again.

4. Click on the **Insert** menu to open it. Three dots after a command indicate that a further selection is available from a dialog box. Click Object... to display the **Insert Object** dialog box.

5. Read the options available then click **Cancel** to close the dialog box.

6. An arrow after a command denotes that another menu will appear. Click **View**, then hold the mouse pointer over Zoom ▶. A further menu appears.

7. Click on **View** again to close the menu.

8. Move the mouse pointer over a button on the **Standard Toolbar** and leave it there for a few seconds. A **ToolTip** appears (an example is shown opposite), showing the name of the button. Read the **ToolTips** for each of the visible buttons.

Exercise 4 - Continued

Note: Chevrons, *, on a toolbar indicate that more buttons are available.*

9.   Toolbars can be moved. To move the **Objects** toolbar on to the same line as the **Standard Toolbar**, move the mouse pointer over the dotted bar, ⬚⬚⬚, at the top of the **Objects** toolbar, until it changes to a four headed arrow, as in the diagram opposite.

10.   Click and hold down the mouse, then drag it across to the right of the **Microsoft Office Publisher Help** button, 🔘, until the toolbar "jumps" on to the line at the right of the **Standard Toolbar**. Notice that chevrons have appeared because some buttons are now hidden. Click on the chevrons to see the hidden buttons. Click away from the buttons to hide them again.

11.   Using the dotted bar, drag the **Objects** toolbar back to its normal position at the left side of the screen.

12.   Select **View | Toolbars** to see the toolbars currently available. The toolbars currently in use have a tick next to them.

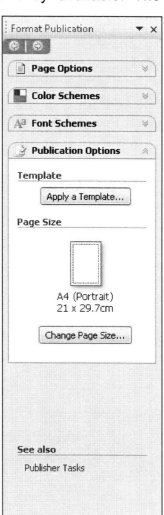

13.   Any listed toolbar can be added to the screen by clicking on it. Click on the **Measurement** toolbar and it appears on the screen.

14.   To remove the **Measurement** toolbar from the screen, select **View | Toolbars** and click **Measurement** again.

15.   If the task pane is not visible at the left of the screen, select **View | Task Pane**. The **Format Publication** task pane appears.

16.   To see the available panes, click the **Other Task Panes** drop down arrow at the right of the **Format Publication** task pane title bar.

17.   Click **Background** to display the task pane that allows various **Backgrounds** to be applied.

18.   In the same way, view the other task panes in turn.

19.   Close the task pane by clicking its **Close** button, ☒.

Note: The task pane will appear when a new publication is opened or started and can be closed if desired.

Exercise 5 - Help

Guidelines:

Publisher has a comprehensive **Help** facility, which can be referred to, either for information or instruction on a particular feature. If a live Internet connection exists *Publisher* will connect to **Office Online** to search for help.

Actions:

1. Select **Help | Microsoft Office Publisher Help** to display the **Publisher Help** window. This contains an area that can be used for a keyword search, or a **Table of Contents** containing help topics organised into different categories.

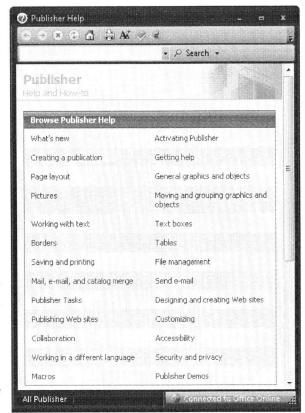

2. Click the **Show Table of Contents** button at the top of the window, if the **Contents** are not displayed on the left.

3. Click the at the left of **Pictures** to reveal the help for this general topic.

4. Select Add pictures and other graphics and general information on the subject appears at the right of the screen, with more specific topics beneath.

5. Scroll down until the **What do you want to do** list appears.

6. Move the mouse over **Insert media from the Clip Organizer** (in blue) until it changes to a pointing hand, Insert media from the Clip Organizer Insert media from the Clip Art task pai and click to display the help. Read the information.

7. Click at the top of the **Publisher Help** window to return to its starting display.

8. In the **Search** box, type **Print** and press **<Enter>**. From the list, scroll down and select **Print crop marks** and read the help options.

9. Click the **Close** button, , at the top of the **Help** window to close **Help**.

Exercise 6 - Text Boxes

Guidelines:

All text in a publication is contained in a **text box**. The text box restricts the area in which the text can be viewed, but there is no limit to the number of boxes which can appear on a page. A box can be very small, or it can fill the page.

Actions:

1. Select the **Text Box** tool, 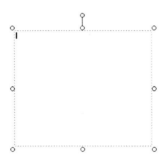, from the **Objects** toolbar.

2. Click and drag a large square in the centre of the page. The text box appears on the page, with the cursor flashing inside it, ready for text to be entered.

3. Notice that the box has small white circles, known as "handles" around it. This shows that it is selected - text can only be entered into a box that is selected.

4. Type in the following text as accurately as possible, but do not worry if you make mistakes:

> **By the time I have completed this Open Learning Guide, I should have mastered the necessary skills to produce impressive desktop publications. I may never have to buy a birthday card again!**

Note: *At this point a message in a yellow speech bubble may appear, because the text will be very small. Press <F9> to zoom in and out to read it. These messages (**tippages**) appear from time to time.*

5. Leave the publication open for the next exercise.

Exercise 7 - Zoom

Guidelines:

When text is entered into a box, it can be so small that it is very difficult to read. To tackle this problem, use the **Zoom** function. This allows you to work closely on an individual object, or to have a view of all items on the page.

Actions:

1. There are several ways to zoom in to and out of a page. The **<F9>** key has already been used, use it now to zoom in to the page, if the text box is not already enlarged.

2. Press **<F9>** again to zoom out.

3. With the text box selected, select **View | Zoom**, then **Selected Objects** to zoom in, so the text box fills most of the screen area.

4. Select **View | Zoom | Whole Page** to zoom out again, so the whole page is visible.

5. It is also possible to zoom in at different percentages of magnification using the menu, but there is a quicker way. Click the **Zoom In** button, , on the **Standard Toolbar** to zoom to **50%**.

Note: If your screen resolution is not set to 1024 x 768 the percentages shown may be different.

6. Click again to zoom to **66%**. Each click of the button zooms in by the next percentage increment shown in the menu options.

7. Zoom out using the **Zoom Out** button, .

8. The **Zoom** box, , on the **Standard Toolbar** can also be used. Click on the drop down arrow at the right of the box and select **10%** from the list.

9. Use the box to zoom in to **400%**.

10. Use any method to zoom to **Whole Page**.

11. Leave the publication open for the next exercise.

Exercise 8 - Positioning and Sizing

Guidelines:

Objects (text boxes, pictures, etc.) can be placed in the correct position on the page using the rulers, which are displayed at the left and top of the screen, and by using the **Object Position** and **Size** areas, which can be found at the bottom of the screen.

Actions:

1. Select the text box created in **Exercise 6** and look at the **Object Position** area at the bottom of the screen, on the **Status Bar**. It shows the exact position of the top right corner of the text box, e.g. 5.000, 11.200 cm.

Note: Don't worry if your text box is sized and positioned differently.

2. The **Object Size** area is to the right of the **Object Position** area, 10.000 x 8.600 cm. Check the size of your text box. Click outside of the text box and move the mouse pointer around the screen. Notice how the figures in the **Object Position** area change.

3. Use the **Object Size** area as a guide, to try to draw a **10cm** x **5cm** text box underneath the first one.

4. Enter the following text: **Objects can be positioned precisely on the page using the Object Position area**.

5. The rulers can be dragged on to the page to make measuring easy. Hold down **<Shift>**, then click and drag the vertical ruler to the right until it touches the closest text box.

6. Hold down **<Shift>** and click and drag the horizontal ruler down until it rests on top of the closest text box. The width of the selected text box is shown on the white area of the ruler. Click on the other text box to see its measurements appear on the ruler. Restore the rulers to their original positions.

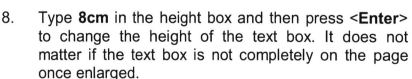

7. Select the second text box, then select **View | Toolbars | Measurement**. Notice how the **x** and **y** boxes show the exact position of the text box and the boxes below show the exact size of the text box.

8. Type **8cm** in the height box and then press **<Enter>** to change the height of the text box. It does not matter if the text box is not completely on the page once enlarged.

9. Close the **Measurement** toolbar and leave the publication open for the next exercise.

Exercise 9 - Closing Publisher

Guidelines:

Publisher can be closed at any time. If the current publication has not been saved, a warning will be displayed asking if it is to be saved.

Actions:

1.   Click on the **File** menu.

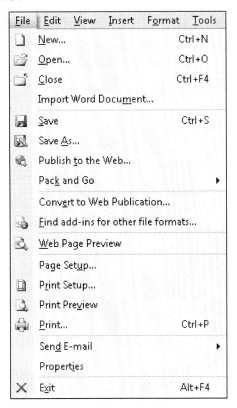

2.   Place the mouse pointer over **Exit** and click once. The following message appears:

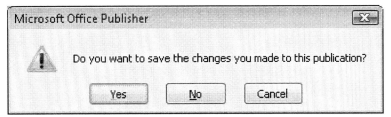

3.   Click **No** to close *Publisher* <u>without</u> saving the publication.

Note: For more information see **Closing a Publication** *in the next section.*

4.   Start *Publisher*. Close the **Getting Started** window (click the black cross below the help question box at the top right) to go directly to an A4 portrait, blank publication.

5.   Close *Publisher* again using the **Close** button, , on the **Title Bar**.

Exercise 10 - Revision

1. Start *Publisher* and a blank publication.

2. Use the **Table of Contents** within **Microsoft Office Publisher Help** to access information from the **Publishing Web Sites** category.

3. Select the help **Prepare, publish and maintain your Publisher Web site**.

4. Now use **Help** to search for **colour text**.

5. Select the **Change the color of text** option and read the information provided.

6. Close the **Help** window.

7. Close the task pane , if displayed.

8. Draw a text box on the page and use the **Measurement** toolbar to resize it to **10cm** x **10cm**, positioning **x** at **5cm** and **y** at **5.75cm**.

9. Close the **Measurement** toolbar and enter the following text, zooming in to read it:

   When it was opened in 1889, the Eiffel Tower was the tallest manmade structure in the world. Designed by a bridge builder, the tower is composed of iron girders held together by bolts, like a giant Meccano set. The feet of the tower are hydraulic, so that it can move slightly in high winds. Barriers have been erected to prevent visitors climbing or falling over the edge.

10. Close *Publisher* <u>without</u> saving the publication.

Section 2

Publications

By the end of this Section you should be able to:

Save, Open and Close Publications

Move the Cursor around a Publication

Select and Edit Text

Use Undo and Redo

Use the Design Checker

Change Page Setup and Print Options

Exercise 11 - Saving a Publication

Guidelines:

A publication must be saved if it is to be used again. There are two main ways to save: **Save As** and **Save**. **Save As** is used to save a newly created publication, i.e. a publication that has not been named. When a publication has already been saved, i.e. been given a name, **File | Save** is used to save/update the current changes in that publication. Use **File | Save As** to change the name or location of an existing publication

Note: *A previously named publication can be saved to the same location under the same name by clicking the* **Save** *button,* *, on the* **Standard Toolbar***. When a new publication is to be saved, selecting* **Save** *also displays the* **Save As** *dialog box.*

Actions:

1.   Start *Publisher* and create a new, A4 portrait, blank publication. This is the default layout to use whenever a blank publication is specified in this guide.

2.   Draw a small text box anywhere on the page. Enter a couple of sentences about yourself and your hobbies.

3.   Select the **File** menu and choose the **Save As** command. The **Save As** dialog box will then appear. The contents of the dialog box will vary between computers, but the diagram below shows an example of how it may look.

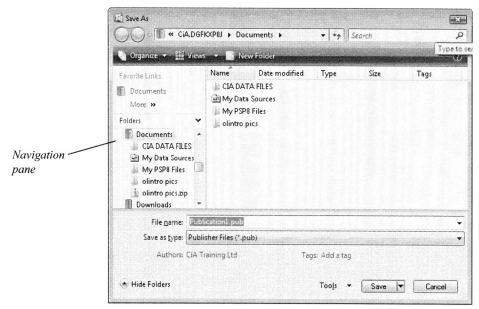

4.   The publication must be given a name. Enter **Personal** in the **File name** box.

Exercise 11 - Continued

Note: A filename can be of any length. Choose a meaningful name but do not use any of the following characters: ><"?:\ /;|.*

5.   The location where the file is to be saved must be shown in the address area at the top of the dialog box. **Documents** is selected by default (publications can be saved to any location on the hard disk or to a floppy disk).

6.   The **Folders** list is in the navigation area, allowing navigation through the folder structure on your computer.

7.   The **Favorite Links** list is another part of the navigation area, allowing quick access to commonly used locations. If **Documents** is not selected, click on it.

8.   Double click on the **CIA DATA FILES** folder then double click on **Open Learning** and finally double click the **Publisher 2007 Introductory Data** folder.

Note: If documents are to be saved elsewhere, select the required location.

9.   Click the **Save** button, [Save ▾], at the bottom right of the dialog box.

*Note: Publisher 2007 files can be opened in Publisher 2003, but it is possible to save a publication in a format that can be opened by very early versions of Publisher; if you want to share files with someone using Publisher 2000, for example. To do this, display the **Save As** dialog box, click on the drop down arrow next to the **Save as type** box and select **Publisher 98 Files** or **Publisher 2000 Files**, then click **Save**.*

10. The **Title Bar** now displays the name of the publication. Leave the publication **Personal** open for the next exercise.

Exercise 12 - Closing a Publication

Guidelines:

A publication can be closed at any time. If it has not been previously saved, or if it has been modified in any way, a prompt to save it will appear.

Actions:

1. The **Personal** publication should still be present on the screen. Move to the end of the text in the text box, press <**Enter**> twice and type in your name.

2. Now select the **File** menu.

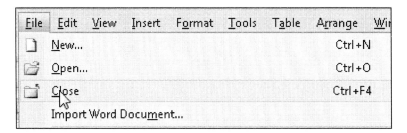

3. Choose the **Close** command.

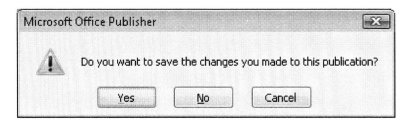

4. The message **Do you want to save the changes you made to this publication?** should appear on the screen. Select **Yes**. The publication is automatically saved to the location specified earlier, overwriting the earlier saved version and then the publication is closed.

Note: *If the publication has just been created and **Yes** is selected, the **Save As** dialog box will appear. **No** closes the publication <u>without</u> saving and **Cancel** returns to the publication.*

Exercise 13 - Opening a Publication

Guidelines:

Once a publication has been created and saved, it can be opened at any time.

Actions:

1. Select **File | Open** to display the **Open Publication** dialog box.

Note: *The **Open Publication** dialog box can be displayed by clicking the **Open** button,* ⌧ *, on the **Standard** toolbar, or by clicking* ⌧ **From File...** *beneath* ***Recent Publications*** *at the right of the **Getting Started** window. To start a new, blank publication, click the **New** button,* ⌧.

2. From the **Navigation Pane** on the left, select the location where the data files are saved.

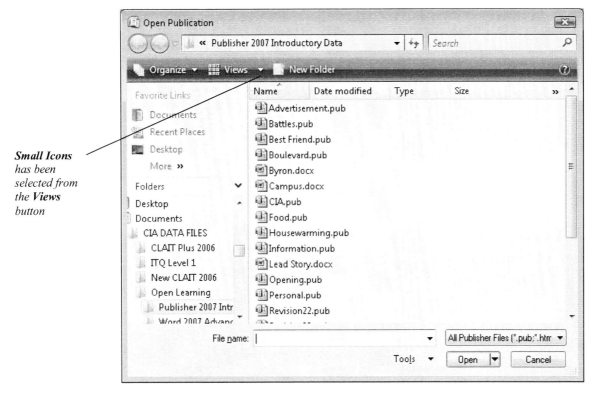

Small Icons
has been
selected from
*the **Views***
button

3. Select the file **Best Friend** from the **File list** on the right and then click **Open**.

4. Use **File | Close** to close the publication, then select **File** from the **Menu Bar**. Recently used publications are listed at the bottom of the **File** menu.

5. Click once on the file name **Personal** to open the file.

6. Now use the **File** menu to open **Best Friend**.

Exercise 13 - Continued

7.   Notice that both publications are open and the **Taskbar** shows a button to represent each.

8.   Click the button for **Personal** to activate that publication and bring it to the front.

9.   Now re-activate **Best Friend**.

10.   Click the **Window** menu. All open publications are listed - the active one has a tick next to it.

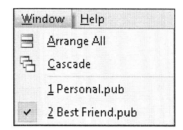

11.   Select **Personal** from the list to make it the active publication.

12.   Close the **Personal** publication.

13.   Close the **Best Friend** publication.

Exercise 14 - Cursor Movement

Guidelines:

The quickest way to move the cursor around a text box is to position the mouse and click the left button, but there are also some useful key movements.

Actions:

1. Click ☐ From File... in the **Getting Started** window to reveal the **Open Publication** dialog box.

2. Select the publication **CIA** and click **Open**.

3. Select the text box and zoom in to see the text.

4. Click in the middle of the word **retail** in the second line of text.

5. Press <**End**>. The cursor is now flashing at the end of the line.

6. Press <**Home**>. Now the cursor is at the beginning of the line.

7. Press <**Ctrl End**> to move to the end of the text.

8. Press <**Ctrl Home**> to move to the start of the text.

9. Place the cursor in the middle of the second paragraph.

10. The cursor keys, ↑, ←, → and ↓, can also be used to move around text. Press each key in turn to move around.

11. These keys can also be used with the <**Ctrl**> key. Press <**Ctrl** →> to move to the next word.

12. Move back one word by pressing <**Ctrl** ←>.

13. Use the key press <**Ctrl** ↓> to move down to the next paragraph.

14. Press <**Ctrl** ↑> to move to the previous paragraph.

15. Leave the publication open for the next exercise.

Exercise 15 - Selecting Text

Guidelines:

Because text has to be selected before it can be edited or formatted, it is important to be familiar with the different selection methods.

Actions:

1. The publication **CIA** should still be open from the previous exercise. If not, open it.

2. Text can be selected by clicking the mouse where the selection is to begin, then dragging the mouse with the button still held down over the area to be selected. When the mouse button is released, the text will be highlighted, showing it has been selected. Select the word **solutions** from the second line of text in the text box by clicking and dragging the mouse across it.

3. Click the mouse once. The text has now been deselected.

4. A quick way to select a word is to move the mouse pointer over the word (it will look like a letter I when over the text) and double click. Select the last word in the text box by double clicking.

Note: A paragraph can be selected by clicking the mouse three times, anywhere within the paragraph.

5. Select all of the text in the box by selecting **Edit | Select All**.

6. Deselect the text.

7. The key press <**Ctrl A**> will also select a full text box. Select the text this way.

8. Close the publication. Do <u>not</u> save any changes if prompted.

Exercise 16 - Editing Text

Guidelines:

It is often necessary to change text after it has been entered, because of errors or omissions.

Actions:

1. Open the publication **Information** and zoom in to read the text.

2. Text is entered where the cursor is flashing (the **Insertion Point**). Move to the end of the text and press the <**Spacebar**> to create a space.

3. Type in the following sentence: **There are also "Pint Questions", where the correct answer wins a pint of guest ale.**

4. In the first article, third paragraph, change **...beam of green light...** to **...beam of violet light...**. Select **green**, then type the replacement text. The highlighted text is replaced.

5. The <**Delete**> key can be used to delete single characters to the right of the cursor. Position the cursor in the last sentence of the same article, before **made** and keep pressing <**Delete**> until the word and full stop have been deleted.

6. The <**Backspace**> key, usually a left pointing arrow above <**Enter**>, deletes text to the left of the cursor. Delete the rest of the sentence using the <**Backspace**> key.

7. Leave the publication open for the next exercise.

Exercise 17 - Undo/Redo

Guidelines:

If something is changed unintentionally, don't despair; the **Undo** and **Redo** commands are there to help. The **Undo** command allows the reversal of some of the last actions performed and **Redo** reverses the **Undo**. These commands work on all objects in a publication.

Actions:

1. Using the publication **Information**, select the title **Dog eats £2.4 million winning lottery ticket** and delete it.

2. Press <**Enter**> to create a new line, then move the cursor up a line.

3. Enter the new title **It's curtains for Chester!**.

4. After reading through the text again, you decide that the first title was better. Click the **Undo** button, [↰ ▾], to delete the new title.

5. Click [↰ ▾] again until the original title is restored.

6. Delete the last sentence in the article.

7. Click [↰ ▾] to undo the deletion.

8. Click the **Redo** button, [↱ ▾] to delete the sentence again.

Note: *These actions can also be performed using the **Edit | Undo** and **Edit | Redo** commands in the menus. The exact wording of these commands changes according to the last action performed.*

9. Save the publication as **Changes** and close it.

Exercise 18 - Design Checker

Guidelines:

It is a good idea to check the design of a publication before attempting to print it. The **Design Checker** feature identifies any possible problems, so that they can be remedied before printing.

Actions:

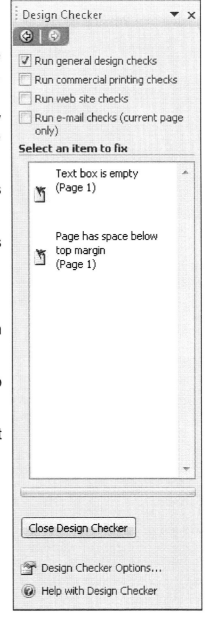

1. With a blank publication on screen, draw a text box in the centre of the page.

2. Select **Tools | Design Checker**. The **Design Checker** task pane appears, showing any possible problems.

3. Move the mouse over **Text box is empty** and click the drop down arrow to see the options.

4. Click **Explain**. Read the help that appears and then close the **Help** window.

5. Click the arrow again. The suggested fix is **Add text** - click it.

6. Type your name in the text box.

7. Notice that the task pane entry has been removed with the solution of the problem.

8. Click on the next problem. There is no automatic fix for this problem.

9. Click **Explain**. The advice is to move the text box.

10. Read the help, then close it.

11. Close the publication <u>without</u> saving.

Exercise 19 - Page Setup

Guidelines:

Page Setup governs the way a publication is printed. The **Publication Layout** for example, can be changed - whether it is printed normally, or like a greeting card. **Paper Size** and **Orientation** – whether it prints in **Portrait**, ☐, or **Landscape**, ☐, can also be changed.

Actions:

1. Open the publication **Best Friend**.

2. Select **File | Page Setup** to display the following dialog box:

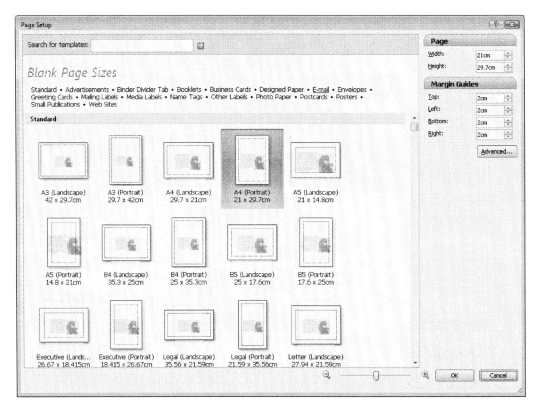

3. Select the **Business Cards** option from the links below **Blank Page Sizes** and notice the changes to the layout that appear in the dialog box. The thumbnails show how the publication will look. The items on this publication aren't suitable for a business card size.

4. Reselect **Standard**.

5. Select **A4 Landscape**.

6. Click **OK**.

7. Leave the publication open for the next exercise.

Exercise 20 - Print Options

Guidelines:

A single copy of a publication can be printed using the **Print** button. However, the **Print** dialog box provides choices on the number of copies printed and the selection of pages in multi-page publications.

Note: Print options for multiple page publications are discussed in the ***Advanced*** *open learning guide for Publisher 2007.*

Actions:

1. Using the publication **Best Friend**, select **File | Print** to display the **Print** dialog box.

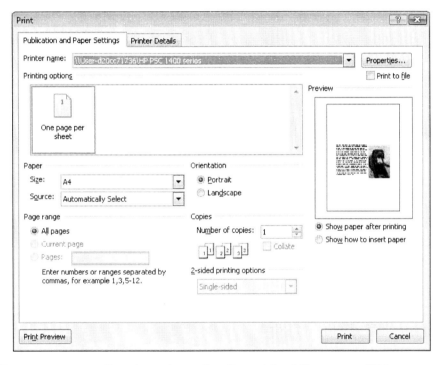

2. The **Page range** option is automatically set to **All pages**. This means that the whole publication will be printed. In this case, there is only one page, so leave the option as it is. The **Number of copies** option is automatically set to **1** (if more than one copy is required, use the arrows at the right to change the number, or type directly into the box). Click **Print** to print the publication.

3. Save the publication as **Orientation** and close it.

4. Open **Tourist**.

5. Click the **Print** button, , to print one copy of the publication, then close it <u>without</u> saving.

Exercise 21 - Revision

The revision exercises from **Section 2** to **Section 8** will use the same file, which will be developed each time to construct a simple community newsletter. Data files containing the publication at the correct stage of development have been provided, so that the revision exercises can still be completed if the guide is not worked through in sequence.

1.   On a blank publication, draw a **5cm** x **5cm** text box.

2.   Using the **Measurement** toolbar, position the text box at **5cm x** and **6cm y**.

3.   Type in the following text:

     Welcome to the first edition of Meadowdene Today, our local community newsletter, to be published weekly. The editor   would   appreciate   interesting   editorial contributions from any members of the community.

4.   Change **Meadowdene Today** to **Meadowdene Weekly**.

5.   Delete **, to be published weekly**, and correct the punctuation where necessary.

6.   Delete **editorial**.

7.   Undo the last deletion.

8.   Draw a second, small text box in the bottom left corner and enter your own name.

9.   Use the **Design Checker** to identify any mistakes and make amendments if you feel they are necessary.

10.   Print a single copy of the publication.

11.   Save it as **Revision Project** and close it.

Note: See the **Answers** at the back of the guide for an idea of how your publication should look.

Section 3

Text Formatting

By the end of this Section you should be able to:

Change Text Fonts, Size and Colour

Apply Text Effects

Apply Drop Caps and Custom Drop Caps

Use Format Painter

Change Alignment, Line and Character Spacing

Apply Tabs

Create Bulleted and Numbered Lists

Check Spelling and Use the Thesaurus

Exercise 22 - Changing Fonts and Font Size

Guidelines:

A **Font** is a type or style of print, such as Arial, Courier, *Rage Italic* and Times New Roman. Changing the font can give a whole new "feel" to a publication: use Comic Sans MS for a greeting card, for example.

Note: The number of fonts available depends on the PC and the printer to which it is connected. If any of the fonts used in the following exercises are not available, select a different one.

The size of text can also be changed to improve the look of a publication – many different text sizes can be used within the same publication. Size is measured in **points**: the larger the point size, the larger the text. When a text box is created, the point size will automatically be set at **10**.

Actions:

1. Open the publication **Food** and zoom in to read the text.

2. This menu needs to be much more eye-catching - applying different fonts will help. Select the first line, **Chez Pascale**.

3. Click on the drop down arrow at the right of the **Font** box, | Times New Roman ▼ |, scroll up the list (which displays a preview of how the font will look) and select **Forte**.

*Note: The font and size can also be changed by selecting **Format | Font** and selecting options before clicking **OK**. Once a font has been used, it is shown at the top of the **Font** drop down list.*

4. Select the following words and apply the same font: **Menu**, **Entrées**, **Main Meals** and **Desserts**.

5. Select the remaining text and change the font to **French Script MT**. This text is now very small. Select all of the text and click the **Increase Font Size** button, | A˄ |, three times.

*Note: The **Decrease Font Size** button, | A˅ |, can be used in the same way to reduce text size.*

6. Select **Chez Pascale**, then click the drop down arrow at the right of the **Size** box, | 14 ▼ | and select **16** to increase the size.

7. Save the publication as **Food2** and close it.

Exercise 23 - Text Effects

Guidelines:

The most common formatting features applied to text are bold, italic and underline:

Bold   to make the text stand out.

Italic   to make the text lean to the right.

Underline   to emphasise text by adding a single line below it.

Text Effects such as **Shadow**, **Outline**, **Emboss** or **Engrave** are also useful tools.

Actions:

1. Open the publication **Best Friend** and zoom in on the text box.

2. Select the first sentence and click the **Bold** button, **B**, to make the text bold.

3. More than one formatting feature can be applied to the same text. Select the next sentence and click the **Italic** button, *I*, then the **Underline** button, **U**. Both features have been applied.

4. Select the next unformatted sentence and select **Format | Font**.

5. From the **Effects** area of the dialog box, click on the check box to the left of **Shadow**, ☑ Shadow, then click **OK** to apply the shadow effect. Increase the zoom to **150%** to see the effect more clearly.

6. In the same way, apply the **Outline** effect to the next unformatted sentence.

7. Select the remaining text, select **Format | Font** and apply the **Engrave** effect then, from the **Font style** drop down box, select **Italic**.

8. Click **OK** to apply the effects.

9. Save the publication as **Effects** and leave it open.

Exercise 24 - Drop Caps

Guidelines:

A **Drop Cap** is the first letter of a paragraph, which is bigger than the rest of the text and either drops below the other rows of text, or is raised partially above them. Drop caps look good in various types of publication, such as newsletters or greeting cards. If the available drop caps are unsuitable, **Custom Drop Caps** can be created.

Actions:

1. Using the publication **Effects**, place the cursor in the first sentence and select **Format | Drop Cap**. The **Drop Cap** dialog box appears.

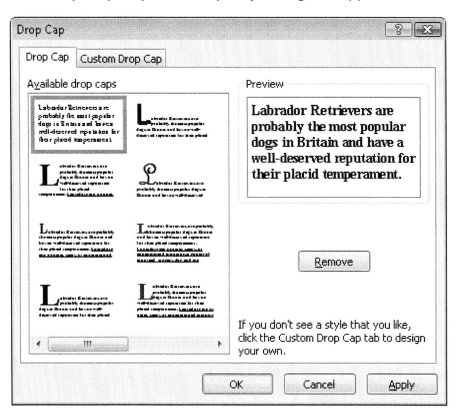

2. Use the scroll bar at the bottom of the **Available drop caps** area to see the choices.

3. Select the second drop cap from the second row, then click **OK** to apply it.

4. Undo the **Drop Cap**.

5. To create a **Custom Drop Cap**, display the **Drop Cap** dialog box again and select the **Custom Drop Cap** tab.

     © CiA Training Ltd 2008

Exercise 24 - Continued

6.   In **Size of letters**, reduce the drop cap to **3** lines high by clicking the ▾ arrow in the **lines high** box.

*Note: The number of letters formatted can also be selected using the **Number of letters** option.*

7.   Uncheck **Use current font** and select the **Mistral** font from the drop down list.

8.   Uncheck **Use current color** and click on the arrow to the right of the **Color** drop down list and choose one of the coloured squares.

9.   Click **OK** to apply the drop cap.

Note: See the Answers at the back of the guide for an idea of how your publication should look.

10.   Print the publication.

11.   Save the publication using the same name and close it.

Exercise 25 - Changing Text Colour

Guidelines:

Text colour is automatically black, but to emphasise parts of a publication, the colour can be changed. Of course, coloured text will only print if the computer is connected to a colour printer.

Actions:

1.   Open the publication **Tourist**. All the text in this publication is black (**Automatic**). Select **Yosemite National Park** from the first line and click the drop down arrow on the **Font Color** button, ![A▾]. A colour palette appears.

2.   Click **More Colors** to display the **Colors** dialog box. Make sure the **Standard** tab is selected. The colours are set out in a honeycomb, with colour groups adjacent to each other.

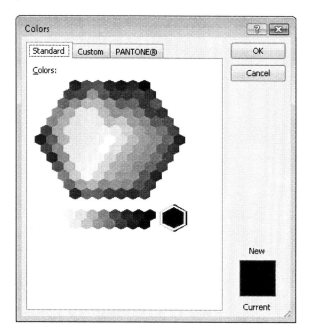

3.   Click on a bright blue hexagon and click **OK**. Click away from the highlighted text to see the effect.

4.   Select the second sentence and change the colour to red. Recently used colours appear on the drop down menu, so they can be used again quickly.

5.   Change the last three lines of text to any shade of green and if you have a colour printer, print a copy.

6.   Close the publication <u>without</u> saving.

   Note: *The **Font** dialog box can also be used to change the colour of text. Select **Format | Font** and select a colour from the **Color** drop down list.*

Exercise 26 - Format Painter

Guidelines:

The **Format Painter** feature can save time when formatting a publication. It copies the formatting applied to one area to another area in a couple of steps.

Actions:

1. Open the publication **Web** and zoom in to read the text.

2. Select the title, **E-Commerce**, make it bold, change the font to **Arial** and the text colour to dark blue.

3. To apply the same formatting to a sub heading, first, make sure the cursor is within the formatted text.

4. Click the **Format Painter** button, [icon]. A paintbrush, [icon], appears next to the cursor when over text.

5. Click and drag to select the **Background** sub heading. Once the mouse is released, it is formatted in exactly the same way, but without the fuss!

6. By double clicking the **Format Painter** button, selected formatting can be applied wherever required. Change the font of the text in the **Background** paragraph to **Comic Sans MS** (or a different font if this is not available), then make it **Italic**, size **8pt**.

7. With this paragraph still highlighted, double click [icon]. Now you can apply the same formatting to several places.

8. Format the rest of the paragraphs, but not the headings, using the **Format Painter** (click and drag the mouse over the text).

9. Click [icon] once more to cancel the **Format Painter**.

Note: The **<Esc>** key also cancels the **Format Painter**.

10. Now use the **Format Painter** to copy the formatting of the **Background** heading to the remaining unformatted headings.

11. Use the **<Esc>** key to end the formatting.

12. Create a text box at the bottom of the page and enter your name.

13. Print the publication, then close it <u>without</u> saving.

Exercise 27 - Alignment

Guidelines:

Alignment refers to how text appears on the screen and the printed page in relation to the margins of the text box. Text can be aligned in four ways: to the **Left**, **Right**, **Centre** or **Justified** (straight left and right margins). Many people prefer to justify text, because of its neat appearance, while **Centre** alignment can be used for flyers, menus, etc.

Actions:

1. Open the publication **Tourist**. Press <**F9**> to see the text more easily. This text is aligned to the **Left**. Alignment is changed using these buttons:

    Align Text Left

    Center

    Align Text Right

    Justify

   Note: It is not necessary to select a whole paragraph before changing its alignment. Just click once anywhere within the paragraph to be aligned, before selecting one of the buttons.

2. Click in the first paragraph, then click the **Align Text Right** button, ☰. See how the paragraph has changed.

3. Centre the last paragraph by clicking within the paragraph, then selecting the **Center** button, ☰.

4. Click in the first paragraph and change its alignment by selecting the **Justify** button, ☰.

5. Select all of the text.

6. Click ☰ to centre the document.

7. Create a text box at the top of the publication and enter your name. Centre the text, make it bold and change the font to any ornate style.

8. Print the publication and close it without saving.

Exercise 28 - Changing Spacing

Guidelines:

Text can be made easier to read if the character, line or paragraph spacing is increased. The normal setting for line spacing is **1** space - other useful spacing is **2** or **1.5** spaces. It is also possible to adjust the spacing between characters (**tracking**), or between pairs of characters (**kerning**). The width of the characters themselves can be changed - this is called **scaling**.

Actions:

1. Open the publication **CIA** and zoom in on the text box to read the text. Use click and drag to select the title text.

2. The easiest way to change spacing is to use the **Measurement** toolbar. Use **View | Toolbars** to display the **Measurement** toolbar. The controls to be used are at the bottom.

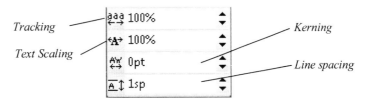

3. Click the up arrow on the **Kerning** box until it reaches **1.5pt**.

4. Change the kerning back to **0pt**, then adjust the **Tracking** of the text to **60%** using the spinners.

5. Click in the first paragraph and increase the line spacing to **1.5sp**.

6. <u>Select</u> the last paragraph and change font to **French Script**. This makes the text difficult to read.

7. Adjust the **Scaling** to **120%** to increase the width of the characters. A slight improvement can be noticed, but this font is not really suitable.

8. Select all of the text and change the font to **Times New Roman 10pt**. Make the **Scaling** and **Tracking 100%**, the **Kerning 0pt** and the **Line Spacing 1sp**.

9. With the text still selected, close the **Measurement** toolbar and select **Format | Character Spacing**.

10. **Stretch** the text to **110%** and click **OK**. This is the **Scaling** option.

Note: All character spacing options can be changed from the dialog box or the toolbar.

Exercise 28 - Continued

11.   Select the next to last paragraph, then select **Format | Paragraph**.

12.   From the **Line spacing** area, select the following options, to change the spacing between the lines and before and after the paragraph to **6pt**.

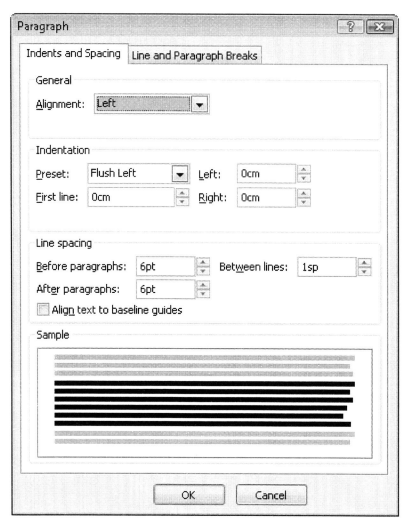

13.   Click **OK** to apply the line and paragraph spacing.

14.   Print the publication and close it <u>without</u> saving.

Exercise 29 - Tabs

Guidelines:

Tabs are an exact measurement for lining up columns of text within a text box. They are often used when creating a list or a table. The **<Tab>** key on the keyboard is usually marked ⇥. Tabs can be set before or after entering text.

Actions:

1. Start a new publication and create a large text box at the top of the page. Zoom in to see the text box more clearly.

2. Tabs are automatically set at 1cm intervals. Press the **<Tab>** key once. Type **Name**, press **<Tab>**, then type **Department** and press **<Enter>** to move down a line.

3. In the same way, enter the information below. Press **<Tab>** before the first column and press it again to move to the second column. Don't worry at this stage if the text doesn't line up properly.

Singh	**Personnel**
Ahmed	**Training**
McPherson	**Sales**
Thompson	**Personnel**

4. Now the tabs can be formatted to make the text line up. First, make sure all of the text is selected, then select **Format | Tabs** to display the **Tabs** dialog box.

5. In the **Tab stop position** box, enter **2cm**. Make sure the **Alignment** is **Left** and the **Leader** is **None**.

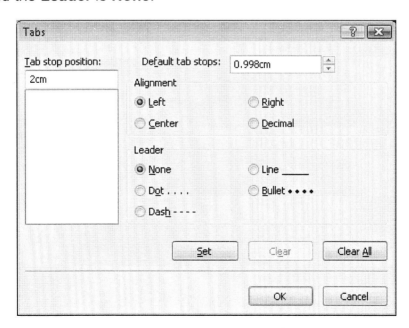

Exercise 29 - Continued

6.   Click **Set** to apply the tab.

7.   Now enter another tab position of **6cm**, but this time change the **Alignment** to **Right** and click **Set**. Click **OK** to return to the publication.

Note: *To remove a tab, select it from the list in the **Tab stop position** box, then click **Clear | OK**.*

8.   Tab settings can be changed using the ruler. Select all of the text.

9.   Notice how the tabs set earlier are marked on the ruler, as in the diagram below.

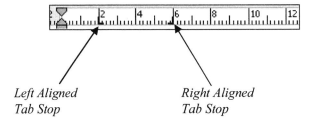

Left Aligned   *Right Aligned*
Tab Stop   *Tab Stop*

10. With the text still selected, click and drag the right **6cm** tab along the ruler to the **8cm** point. The text moves to the new tab.

11. With the text still selected, select **Format | Tabs**.

12. Click on the **8cm** tab in the list and change the **Alignment** to **Left**.

Note: *If you have not been precise in step **9**, the list may show a tab measurement slightly less or slightly more than **8cm**. This doesn't matter, just select this tab.*

13. Click **Set**, then **OK**. The text in this column is now aligned to the left.

14. Save the publication as **Departments**.

15. Close the publication.

Exercise 30 - Applying Bullets and Numbering

Guidelines:

Bullets (small symbols) and **numbers** can be added to lists and paragraphs, making for easier reading and reference. When bullets or numbers are added, an indent is also applied, separating the text from the bullets/numbers and improving its appearance.

Actions:

1. Open the publication **Web** and select the text box. Zoom in to see the text, then select the list of four **Points to Note** at the bottom.

2. Click the **Bullets** button, on the **Formatting** toolbar to apply the bullets.

3. In this case, numbering would be more effective. With the list selected, click.

4. Click again to remove the numbering.

5. With the list selected, select **Format | Bullets and Numbering**. Make the selections shown in the diagram below.

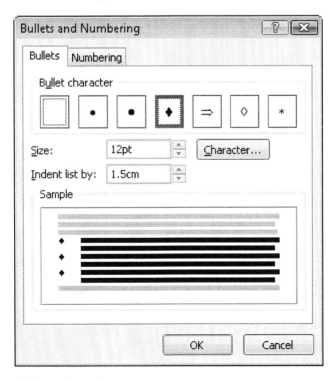

6. Click **OK** to apply the bullets.

Exercise 30 - Continued

7.   With the list selected, display the **Bullets and Numbering** dialog box.

8.   This time choose the **Numbering** tab and make selections as below.

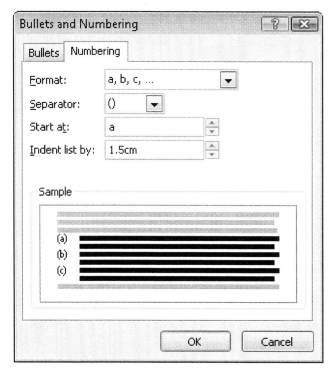

9.   Click **OK** to apply the numbering.

10. Close the publication <u>without</u> saving.

11. Bullets and numbers can also be applied as data is entered. Start a blank publication.

12. Draw a text box on the page. To automatically apply bullets, type * then press **<Tab>**.

13. Type in **Item 1**, then press **<Enter>**. The currently selected bullet is automatically applied to the next line.

14. Type in **Item 2** and press **<Enter>**. Continue doing this until there are 5 items in the list.

15. Press **<Enter>** twice to stop the automatic bullets.

16. Automatic numbering is applied similarly, but with using **1** Instead of *. Create a list of 3 numbered items.

17. Close the publication <u>without</u> saving.

Exercise 31 - Spell Checking and Thesaurus

Guidelines:

Text is automatically checked for spelling and repeated words. Spelling errors are underlined with a jagged red line. *Publisher* also contains a thesaurus, to help suggest alternatives for words that aren't quite right.

*Note: Words which are not in the dictionary are marked as spelling mistakes, so some proper names, e.g. of people or places, will be underlined in red. These can be ignored, or added to the dictionary. Words used incorrectly such as **horse** instead of **house** will not be highlighted (because they <u>are</u> words in the dictionary).*

Actions:

1. On a new blank publication draw a text box at the top of the page.

2. Type in your name and address, then leave a line and enter the following text:

    This is an exercise to check speling. Publisher will highligt my misteaks in red.

3. Position the cursor at the beginning of the text and select **Tools | Spelling | Spelling** to display the **Check Spelling** dialog box.

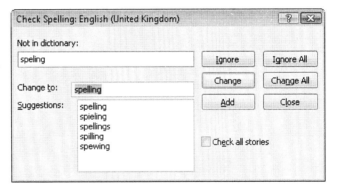

Note: The first word found in your publication may be different, if any part of your name or address is not recognised.

4. An alternative is shown in the **Change to** box and more **Suggestions** are shown below. If the alternative is correct, click **Change** to correct the spelling. If not, choose an option from **Suggestions**. The next error is shown.

5. Alternatively, if you want the word to remain the way it appears, click **Ignore**.

*Note: Change all uses of an incorrect word by clicking **Change All**. To check spelling for all text boxes in a publication, make sure the **Check all stories** option is selected.*

6. Work through the rest of the text, making any appropriate changes (it may be necessary to type the correct entry into **Change to**) and click **OK** when finished.

Exercise 31 - Continued

Note: A word underlined in red can be corrected by clicking on it with the right mouse button and correcting the spelling from the suggestions on the shortcut menu.

7. Read through the text to make sure there are no further mistakes.

Note: Publisher will not recognise the incorrect use of correctly spelled words, e.g. **Please contract me on 0191 549 5002.**

8. Close the publication <u>without</u> saving.

9. Open the publication **Boulevard** and zoom in on the lowest text box.

10. Place the cursor in the text box within the word **structure** and select **Tools | Language | Thesaurus**.

11. Alternate words are listed. The list may be grouped under headings representing different possible meanings of the selected word. In this example the headings are **arrangement**, **construction** and **arrange**.

Note: The ***Thesaurus*** *may not always be able to make a suggestion.*

12. Under **construction**, move the cursor over the word **assembly** and click the drop down arrow to the right. Click **Insert**.

13. Notice how the text has been amended. Adjust the spacing if necessary.

14. Place the cursor within the word **slightly** and press **<Shift F7>** to refresh the thesaurus pane.

15. Click the drop down arrow for **a little** from the suggested synonyms for **somewhat** and click **Insert**.

16. The text is amended again.

17. Close **Boulevard** <u>without</u> saving.

Exercise 32 - Revision

1. Open the **Revision Project** publication (if the previous revision was not completed, open **Revision21** from the data files and save it immediately as **Revision Project**).

2. Zoom in on the top text box.

3. Select all of the text and change the font to **High Tower Text**.

4. Increase the size once using $\boxed{A^{\hat{}}}$, change the text colour to red and **Emboss** the text.

5. Apply a drop cap to the text box using the first style on the third row.

6. Increase the **Tracking** of the text to **119.1%** by typing the value into the box.

7. Draw a third text box, measuring exactly **7.5 x 3.3cm**, in the bottom right corner of the page.

8. Type in **Contacts**, press <**Enter**> twice to create a space and enter the following list, pressing <**Tab**> before each job title:

    Anna Borlick   **Editor**

    Phil Lemmin   **Events Organiser**

    Peter Rowte   **Art Director**

9. Set a **Left** tab for the list at **3cm**.

10. Change the line spacing of the list only to **1.25 sp**.

11. **Bullet** the list and change the colour to **dark blue**, then change the font of all text in the text box to **Cooper Black**.

12. Change the size of **Contacts** to **12pt** and its colour to **gold**.

13. Copy the format of **Contacts** to your name in the text box opposite. Don't worry at this stage if all of the text is not visible.

14. Check the spelling for all text boxes.

15. Save the publication as **Revision Project**, overwriting the original file if prompted, and close it.

Note: *See the Answers at the back of the guide for an idea of how your publication should look.*

Section 4

Working with Text Boxes

By the end of this Section you should be able to:

Change Text Box Properties

Move/Resize a Text Box

Use Layout Guides

Apply Borders, Border Art and Shadow

Apply Colour and Fill Effects to a Text Box

Import Text Files

Connect Text Boxes

Work with Columns, Sidebars and Callouts

Use the Scratch Area

Exercise 33 - Text Box Margins

Guidelines:

Text box margins create space between the text and the edges of a text box. They are controlled using the **Format Text Box** dialog box.

Actions:

1. Open the publication **CIA** and select the text box.

2. Zoom in to read the text and select **Format | Text Box** and the **Text Box** tab.

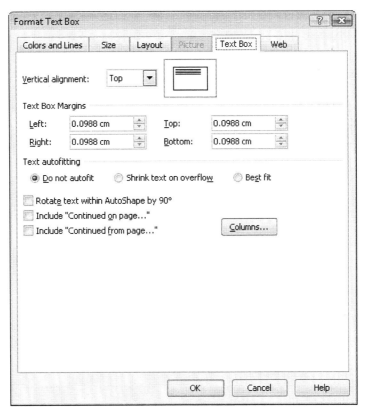

3. To increase the space between the edge of the text box and the text, select the number in the **Left Text Box Margin** box and type **0.75cm**.

Note: This is changing the margins in the text box only.

4. Press **<Tab>** to move to the **Top** margin box and enter **0.75cm**.

5. In the same way, change the **Right** and **Bottom** margins to **0.75cm**. Click **OK**. Notice how the text has moved away from the text box frame.

6. Select **Format | Text Box** and the **Text Box** tab again.

7. Change all of the margins to **0.2cm** to reduce the white space.

8. Save the publication as **CIA2** and close it.

Exercise 34 - Moving and Resizing Text Boxes

Guidelines:

A text box can be moved to any position on a page, but it must first be selected (have its handles visible). A text box is moved by positioning the mouse over an edge, not a handle, and clicking and dragging. To change the size of a text box, the mouse must be moved over a handle before clicking and dragging.

Actions:

1.   Open the publication **Best Friend** and select the text box beside the picture.

2.   Don't zoom in, as the whole page should be in view.

3.   To move the text box, move the mouse over any of its edges until a **Move** pointer, appears.

4.   Click and drag the text box down to the bottom left corner of the page, then release the mouse.

5.   Now move the mouse over the top right handle of the text box until a **Resize** pointer, appears.

Note: *Pointers may look different if the Publisher is running under Windows XP.*

6.   Click and drag upwards and to the right until the text box fills most of the page.

7.   Move the mouse over the middle handle at the top of the text box until appears and reduce the size of the text box to about half a page.

Note: *Notice how the text is always wrapped around the picture.*

8.   Use the top right corner handle to reduce the size of the text box to a quarter of a page.

9.   will appear if the text box has been made too small to accommodate the text. If necessary, increase the size of the text box using the middle handle at the top until disappears.

10.   Now move the text box to the top of the page.

11.   Leave the publication open.

Exercise 35 - Margins and Layout Guides

Guidelines:

Margin and **layout guides** help to line up objects on the page. The blue dotted lines around the page of every publication are the guides, but more can be added to make the positioning more precise. Layout guides are not printed. While margins can be set on the page, text and picture frames can be placed outside them. You must, therefore, be careful when placing boxes making sure they will appear within the printed area for your particular printer.

Note: *Baseline guides, available from the same dialog box as the other guides, can also be used to help align lines of text, but they are not used in this guide.*

Actions:

1. Using the publication **Best Friend**, select **Arrange | Layout Guides** to display the **Layout Guides** dialog box.

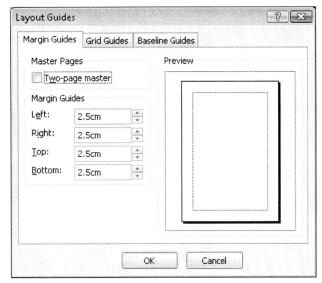

2. Normally, the only guides showing are the margin guides around the edge of the page. These can be altered, but remember that boxes or frames may overlap them.

3. Click and drag across the **Left Margin Guide** value to select it. Type in **5**.

4. For the **Right Margin Guide**, click on the up arrow and change the value to **4.5**.

5. Change the **Top Margin Guide** by clicking and dragging across the value and typing in **8**.

6. Click **OK**. Notice how the boxes already placed on the page are unaffected, but the **Margin Guides** have changed to the values entered. This has changed the page margins rather than text box margins.

7. Set all margins back to **2.5cm**.

8. View the **Layout Guides** dialog box again and select the **Grid Guides** tab.

Exercise 35 - Continued

9. A grid can be created on the page to help line up objects. Change the number of **Columns** to **4** using the up spinner at the right of the **Columns** box.

10. Change the number of **Rows** to **6**. Notice how the **Preview** changes.

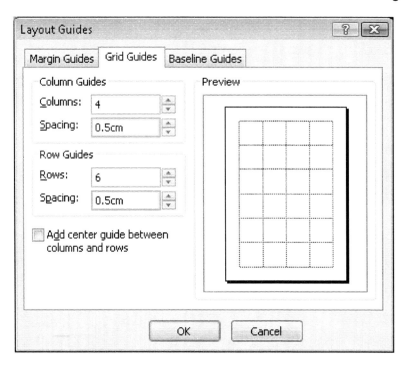

11. Click **OK**, then select **Arrange | Snap** and make sure that **To Guides** has a tick next to it, but **To Ruler Marks** does not. This means that when the text box is being dragged, it will be pulled when near a guide, so that it is in line with it.

12. With the text box selected, move it very slowly around the page. This feature can be very subtle, so watch closely to see how the text box behaves when near a guide.

13. Select **Arrange | Snap** and remove the check from **To Guides**. Now observe the behaviour of the text box as it is moved around the page to see if you can notice the slight difference.

14. Turn **Snap | To Guides** on and select **Arrange | Layout Guides**, then from **Grid Guides** change the number of **Columns** to **6** and the number of **Rows** to **8**. Click **OK**.

15. Move the picture frame around the page in a similar way to the text box. The more guides there are on the page, the more precise the positioning of objects can be.

16. Close the publication <u>without</u> saving.

Exercise 36 - Applying Borders and Shadow

Guidelines:

A border can be added to a text box to make it stand out from the rest of the page.

Actions:

1.   Open the publication **Boulevard**.

2.   Select the lower text box and zoom in to see it more clearly.

3.   Click the **Line/Border Style** button, ☰ on the **Formatting** toolbar. A drop down menu appears.

4.   Select **More Lines** to display the **Format Text Box** dialog box.

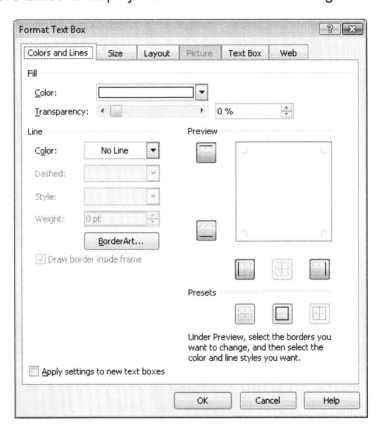

5.   From **Line Color**, select **purple** from the grid. Increase the **Weight** of the line to **2pt**.

6.   Note the preview. Click **OK** to close the dialog box and apply the border.

7.   Picture borders can be created around a text box. This type of border is known as **Border Art**. Zoom out and select the **Visit the landmarks of Paris** text box.

Exercise 36 - Continued

8.   Click ☰ and select **More Lines**, then click the **BorderArt** button.

9.   Scroll down the list of available borders and select the **Flowers...Pansy** art.

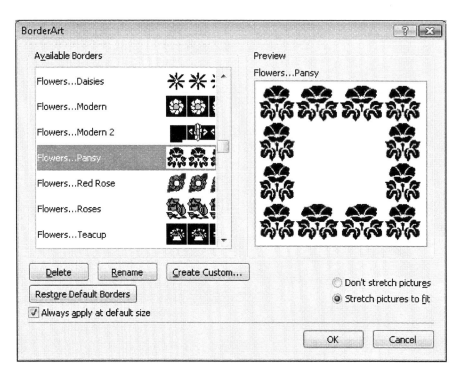

10.   Click **OK** and change the **Weight** to **12pt**.

11.   Click on the **Color** drop down list and pick one of the displayed colours from the list.

12.   Click **OK** to apply the border.

13.   The text box is now too small to accommodate the text. Increase the size of the box until all of the text can be seen.

Note: *To remove a border, select the text box, select **Format | Text Box** and the **Colors and Lines** tab. Select **No Line** from **Line Color**, then click **OK**.*

14.   Select the lower text box. To add a shadow to this box, click the **Shadow Style** button, 🔲 and choose **Style 10**.

Note: *Shadows and borders can be applied to any text box. See the **Drawing Objects** exercise in **Section 8** for instructions on how to apply a custom shadow.*

15.   To remove the shadow, click the button again and choose **No Shadow**.

16.   Save the publication as **Borders** and close it.

Exercise 37 - Filling Text Boxes

Guidelines:

Colour can be added to an entire text box, so that it stands out on the page. **Fill effects** are used to apply a pattern or shading effect to a text box.

Actions:

1. Open the publication **Tourist** and move the text box to the top left corner of the page.

2. Click the down arrow on the **Fill Color** button, , on the **Formatting** toolbar and from the menu, select **More Fill Colors** to display the palette. Select a pale green from the grid, then click **OK** to apply the colour.

3. With the text box selected, click again, display the palette and select black from the grid then click **OK**. The text cannot be seen.

4. Change the text colour (press <**Ctrl A**> to select all of the text) to yellow and centre the text.

5. Create a small text box at the bottom of the page and enter your name.

6. Change the font to **Harrington 16pt** bold and centre the text. Resize the text box so that your name is centred vertically.

7. To make the text box stand out, a special effect is to be applied to it. Click , then select **Fill Effects** from the menu.

8. Select the **Gradient** tab.

9. From **Colors**, select **Two colors**. Click the drop down list for **Color 1** and select **More colors**.

10. Select a mid blue and click **OK**. Notice how the **Sample** reflects the choice.

11. Now click the drop down arrow on the **Color 2** box, select **More colors** and choose **purple**. If you used the honeycomb click **OK** to see the effect.

12. From **Shading styles** select **From center** and click **OK** to return to the publication.

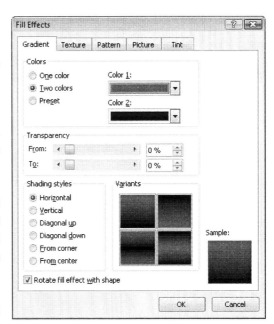

Exercise 37 - Continued

13. Now draw a small text box at the top right of the page and zoom in to see it clearly.

14. Type in the word **Patterns** and change the font to **Castellar**.

15. Centre the text and use $\boxed{\text{A}}$ to increase the text to fill the text box.

16. Open the **Fill Effects** dialog box, then select the **Pattern** tab.

17. The selection of patterns is displayed. Select the **Horizontal brick** (row 4, column 6).

18. Click the **Foreground** drop down arrow. The **recent colors** are displayed in the menu. Select the same blue used for the gradient effect.

19. In the same way, select purple as the background.

20. Click **OK** to apply the effect.

21. Create a text box at the bottom right of the page and enter the date.

22. Click $\boxed{\text{🖌}}$, then select **Fill Effects** and the **Tint** tab. A tint is a colour mixed with white and a shade is a colour mixed with black.

23. Click the **Base color** drop down arrow and choose **More Colors** and then a green option. Click **OK**.

24. A graded selection of green tints and shades is now displayed in the dialog box. Choose the sample described as **70% Tint** (look at the text beneath the colours to make sure the correct option is selected), then click **OK**.

25. Give the text box a **2pt Black** border.

26. Print the publication.

27. Close it <u>without</u> saving.

Exercise 38 - Importing Text Files

Guidelines:

Text, which already exists in another location, can be inserted into a publication. Once a text box has been drawn, it is easy to insert a file.

Actions:

1. On a new publication, in **Portrait** orientation, draw a large text box to cover the top two thirds of the page.

2. With the text box selected, click **Insert | Text File** to display the **Insert Text** dialog box.

3. Make sure the address area shows the location where the data files are saved, i.e. **Documents\CIA DATA FILES**, etc. and that the **Files of type** box shows **All Text Formats**.

4. Click on **Byron** to select the file.

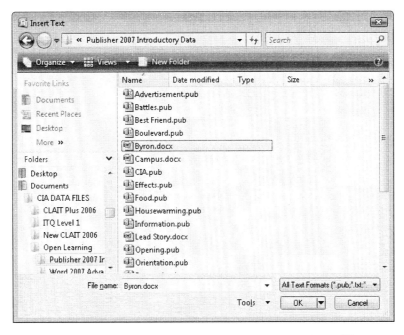

5. Click **OK**. The message **Publisher is converting this file** appears. The file is inserted into the text box.

6. Select the text and change the font to **Book Antiqua**, then justify the text.

7. Resize the text box so that the text fits it neatly and move it halfway down the page.

8. Add a border and shadow to the text box and fill it with a colour of your choice.

9. Leave the publication open for the next exercise.

Exercise 39 - Connecting Text Boxes

Guidelines:

To make text in a text box flow from one place in a publication to the next, it can be placed in text boxes and then the text boxes can be linked, even if the locations aren't next to each other. This means, for example, a story starting on page 1 of a newsletter can be linked directly to the end of the story on page 4.

Actions:

1.   Using the publication from the last exercise, reduce the size of the text box by half.

2.   Move it to the top of the page.

3.   Zoom in to see the text box. Because the text box is not big enough to show all of the text, the **Text in Overflow** button, A···· appears at the bottom.

4.   Draw a second text box, about half the size of the page, beneath the first, then select the first text box again.

Note: *The **Connect Text Boxes** toolbar,* should be displayed. *If not, select **View | Toolbars | Connect Text Boxes**.*

5.   Click **Create Text Box Link**, ⊂⊃ and move the mouse pointer over the first text box, containing text. It changes to . The "pitcher" contains the text which does not fit into the text box.

6.   Move the pitcher over the empty text box and it changes to . Click once to "pour" the extra text into the new text box.

7.   The second text box has a **Go to Previous Text Box** button, ⬅▢, at the top. Move the mouse over it and the pointer changes to a pointing hand. Click on it to move back to the first text box.

8.   Now the first text box has a **Go to Next Text Box** button, ▢➡, at the bottom. Click it to move to the second text box.

9.   The link is automatic. Reduce the size of the first box and notice how more text flows into the second.

Note: *If the **Break Forward Link** button, is clicked when the first text box is selected, the connection will be broken and the text removed from the second text box. The buttons on the **Connect Text Boxes** toolbar can also be used to move between text boxes.*

10.   Save the publication as **Links** and close it.

Exercise 40 - Columns

Guidelines:

Columns divide the text vertically into sections within its text box. This is a different way of presenting text, which would look really effective in a newsletter, for example.

Actions:

1. Open **Information**, select the text box and zoom to **66%**.

2. Select **Format | Text Box** and the **Text Box** tab.

3. Click Columns... and change the **Number of columns** to **2**.

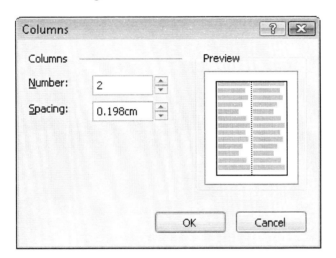

4. Click **OK** then **OK** again to divide the text box into two columns.

5. Display the **Format Text Box** dialog box again and click the **Columns** button.

6. Increase the number of columns to **3** and click **OK** and **OK** again.

7. Change the size of the text box until the text is evenly shared between the columns and use the layout guides to centre the text box on the page.

8. Create a text box at the bottom of the page and enter your name. Centre the text and add a **1pt** red border.

9. Print the publication, then close it <u>without</u> saving.

Exercise 41 - Sidebars and Callouts

Guidelines:

A **Sidebar** (or **Side Heading**) is additional text related to the main body of text; it usually appears in a narrow column to the left or right of the page. The information appearing in this text box would normally hold additional information or interesting points, which would add to the reader's enjoyment but would not be necessary for the understanding of the main text.

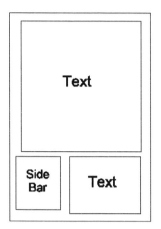

A sidebar would usually be visually similar to the main body of text, with the same font and size, but may be made different by adding a border or shading to the text box. A sidebar can be added by inserting a text box in the desired place and formatting it slightly differently. An example of a sidebar is shown in the upper diagram on the right.

Callout boxes (or **pull quotes**) are parts of text from the main body of text, which are copied and emphasised to attract the reader's attention to specific points. A callout box may contain quotes from the text using a larger font and the box may include shading and a border. An example of a callout box is shown in the lower diagram on the right.

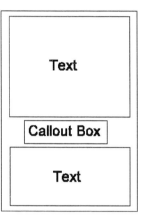

Actions:

1. Open the publication **Sharks2**. The text **cut human skin** is in a callout box. Notice that the original text is in the paragraph next to the callout box.

2. Close the publication <u>without</u> saving.

3. From the **Getting Started** window select **Newsletters**. Double click on the **Modular** design.

4. Zoom in on the tall thin text box at the left. This is a **sidebar**.

5. Close the publication <u>without</u> saving.

6. Open the publication **Information** and apply 2 columns to the text box.

7. Resize the text box to **11.5cm x 21.5cm** using the **Measurement** toolbar.

8. Ensure the right edge of the text box touches the right page margin and move it to the bottom of the page.

Exercise 41 - Continued

9.   To create a sidebar, first draw a text box measuring **4.3cm** x **3.4cm** and position it at the left of the page, in the centre.

10. Enter the following bulleted text:

- **Alien Abduction**

- **Lottery Loser**

- **Coffee Morning**

- **Lydia Pann Visit**

- **Quiz Prizes**

11. Format the list as **Impact 12pt** and **red**.

12. Apply a **1½pt** black border and fill the text box with pale blue.

13. At the top of the page draw a text box measuring **16cm** x **3cm** and type in **Top Stories** and centre it.

14. Format this text as **Impact 72pt** and apply a **2¼pt** black border to the text box.

15. Save the publication as **News** and close it.

Exercise 42 - The Scratch Area

Guidelines:

The **Scratch Area** is the grey area around the page. It is used to store text and pictures before they are placed on the page. Objects can be worked on in the **Scratch Area** before their final position is decided. If objects are left on the **Scratch Area** when saving the publication, they will still be available when it is opened again.

Actions:

1. Open the publication **Boulevard** and close the task pane so that as much of the page as possible is in view.

2. Select the **WordArt**, **Boulevard Tours**, at the top of the page and drag it to the left, on to the **Scratch Area**.

3. Drag the other text boxes and the picture off the page, leaving only the background, until it looks like the diagram below.

4. Zoom out to **10%** to see how far the **Scratch Area** extends.

5. Zoom to **33%** and move the picture back on to the page. Select the text box containing the most text and zoom in.

6. Change the font to **Old English Text MT** and resize the text box if necessary.

7. Save the publication as **Scratch** and close it.

8. Open **Scratch**. The objects are still where they were left on the **Scratch Area**.

9. Close the publication <u>without</u> saving.

Exercise 43 - Revision

1. Open the **Revision Project** publication (if the previous revision was not completed, open **Revision32** from the data files and save it immediately as **Revision Project**), and use **Layout Guides** to set **Grid Guides** of, **4** columns and **5** rows.

2. Select the text box at the top of the page, change the left and right margins to **0.5cm**, justify the text and resize the text box just enough to accommodate the text.

3. Select the **Contacts** text box at the bottom of the page and fill it with a two colour **Gradient** effect. Make the **Color 1** light blue and **Color 2** dark blue.

4. Apply a **2pt** blue border to the text box.

5. Fill the text box containing your name with a **20% tint** of a dark blue.

6. Apply a **1pt** blue border and a shadow.

7. Fill the top text box with a **30%** tint of purple and apply **Border Art - Flowers...Tiny**, changing the **Border Art** colour to purple.

8. Change the text colour to dark blue.

9. Resize the text box to accommodate the text and move it to the top right corner.

10. Draw a text box measuring **12cm** x **6.5cm** in the centre of the page. Align the bottom of the box with the third horizontal grid line.

11. Import the text file **Lead Story** into the text box.

12. Change the font to **Tempus Sans ITC**.

13. Fill the text box with a **30%** tint of purple, apply a **1pt** purple border.

14. Apply 2 columns to the text and resize the text box if necessary to balance the columns.

15. Embolden the title, **History of Meadowdene** and justify all of the text in the text box.

16. Save the changes to the **Revision Project** publication, overwriting the original if prompted, and close it.

Note: See the Answers at the back of the guide for an idea of how your publication should look.

Section 5

Tables

By the end of this Section you should be able to:

Insert and Delete a Table

Enter Text

Format Cells

Change Column Width and Row Height

Insert Rows and Columns

Merge and Split Cells

Create Cell Diagonals

Exercise 44 - Inserting a Table

Guidelines:

Although tabs can be used to organise rows and columns of information, it can often look much more effective when presented as a table. Tables are made up of cells, like spreadsheets. The cells form **rows**, which run from left to right, and **columns** which run from top to bottom. Text stays in a cell, although it can spill over one line. Tabs can be used in a cell, but are only useful when the text fits on one line.

Tables are not difficult to create; they can be moved and resized in the same way as other objects.

Actions:

1. Start a new publication.

2. Click **Insert Table**, ⬜, from the **Objects** toolbar.

3. Tables are placed on the page in the same way as text boxes. Click and drag a table measuring about **10cm** x **10cm** on the page. When the mouse is released, the **Create Table** dialog box appears.

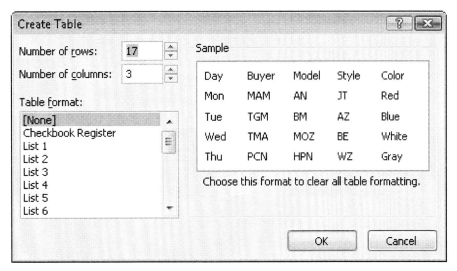

4. Change the **Number of rows** to **6** and the **Number of columns** to **3**. Leave the **Table format** the same, i.e. **[None]**.

5. Click **OK** to create the table.

6. Leave the publication open for the following exercise.

Exercise 45 - Entering Text

Guidelines:

Once a table has been created, it is simple to enter text and to move around it. It is probably easier to type the text into the table first and then format the table, i.e. correct column widths and/or row heights.

Actions:

1. The table is created within the frame drawn earlier. Zoom in to see the table properly.

2. Starting in the top left cell, enter the following information:

Note: *When entering information in a table, use <**Tab**> to move forwards and <**Shift Tab**> to move backwards. The cursor keys can also be used to move around. Do not use <**Enter**> unless a new line is needed within the same cell, e.g. as in an address.*

Make	Model	Colour
Renault	Megane	Red
Vauxhall	Astra	Black
Ford	Mondeo	Green
VW	Golf	White
Fiat	Punto	Silver

3. Save the publication as **Motors**.

4. Leave it on screen for the next exercise.

Exercise 46 - Formatting Cells

Guidelines:

Before cells can be formatted they must be selected.

Actions:

1. Select the top row of the table by moving the mouse to the left of the row outside the table until it changes to an arrow, →. Click once to select the row.

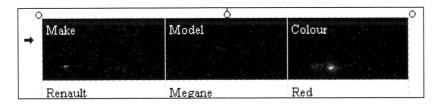

2. Make the text bold, red and centred.

3. Change the font of this text to **Comic Sans MS** and increase the size to **12pt**.

4. Select the first column by moving the mouse above it until the arrow appears. Click to select the column.

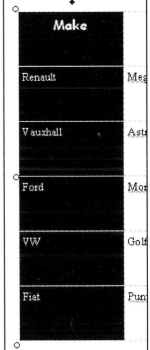

5. Centre this text and change the font to **Comic Sans MS**.

6. Click and drag above the remaining two columns to select them. Multiple rows can also be selected in this way.

7. Repeat step 5.

Note: *Cells can also be selected by clicking and dragging within the table. Alternatively, select the relevant area using the menus:* **Table | Select | Table / Column / Row / Cell.**

8. Double click on the table frame to display the **Format Table** dialog box and add a **1pt Red** border.

9. Select the top row and click the **Fill Color** button, 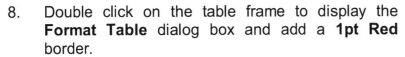. Fill this row with pale grey. Click away from the top row to see the shading.

10. Fill the rest of the table with a **20% tint** of dark green.

11. Save the changes to the table and leave it open for the next exercise.

Exercise 47 - Deleting a Table

Guidelines:

Just as text can be deleted, it is possible to delete an entire table. To delete a table, it must first be selected.

Actions:

1.　Make sure the **Motors** table is selected.

2.　Click and drag inside the table to select the contents.

3.　Press <**Delete**> to remove the information.

4.　To delete the entire table, select it so that its handles are showing.

5.　Select **Edit | Delete Object** to remove the table.

6.　Click **Undo,** 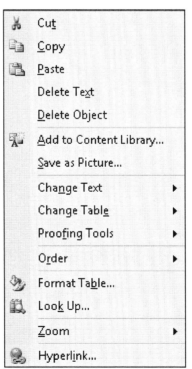, to display the table again.

7.　To delete the table again, right click on it with the mouse. A shortcut menu appears.

✂	Cu**t**
🗐	**C**opy
📋	**P**aste
	Delete Te**x**t
	Delete Object
🗐	**A**dd to Content Library...
	Save as Picture...
	Cha**n**ge Text ▶
	Change Tab**l**e ▶
	Proo**f**ing Tools ▶
	O**r**der ▶
🖉	Format Ta**b**le...
📖	Loo**k** Up...
	Zoom ▶
🌐	Hyper**l**ink...

8.　Select **Delete Object** from the shortcut menu.

9.　Close the publication <u>without</u> saving any changes.

*Note: The table and contents can be deleted at the same time by clicking on the edge of a table to select the entire table (the cursor should not be seen anywhere within the table) and pressing <**Delete**>.*

Exercise 48 - Change Column Width and Row Height

Guidelines:

Once all data has been entered into a table, the size of the cells may need to be changed, so that the information fits properly and looks effective. Column width and row height can also be changed.

Actions:

1. Open the publication **Advertisement**. This publication contains a table and two text boxes.

2. Select the table and zoom in to see it clearly.

3. To make the columns just wide enough to fit the text, move the mouse over the line between the first and second columns until it becomes ◀║▶.

4. Click and drag the mouse to the left until the text fits the column neatly.

5. Now adjust the width of the remaining columns in the same way.

6. Move the table into the centre of the page.

7. To adjust the row height evenly, click and drag the mouse down the left outside edge of the table and select all of the rows.

8. Now move the mouse over the border of any row until the **Adjust** pointer, ⬚ appears.

9. Click and drag downwards to make the rows taller.

10. Now click and drag upwards to return them to their original size.

11. To improve the look of the table, centre all of the data it contains.

12. Change the font colour to white and embolden all of the text. Increase the size of the top row to **12pt**.

13. Add a two colour gradient **Fill Effect** to the table, with the **Color 1** as dark blue and **Color 2** as turquoise.

14. Double click on the table frame and add a border using the **Lightning BorderArt**, **6pt**.

15. In each text box, centre and increase the size of the text until it is the width of the frame.

16. Resize the text boxes so that the text appears vertically centred.

17. Leave the publication open for the next exercise.

Exercise 49 - Inserting Rows and Columns

Guidelines:

If more information is to be added to a table, extra rows and columns can be inserted as required. These can be added to the edges of the table, or between existing rows and columns.

Actions:

1. Using the **Advertisement** table, click in the twelfth row (**Internet Appreciation**).

2. Select **Table | Insert | Rows Above**. A new row is inserted above the selected cell.

3. Enter the following information into this row:

    Visual Basic   **Introductory**   **2 days**

4. Move the bottom text box away from the table.

5. Click in the **time to Complete** column and select **Table | Insert | Columns to the Right**.

Note: *Use the **Table | Insert...** command to insert rows or columns wherever required.*

6. Enter the column heading **Certificate** in the top cell.

7. Enter **Yes** in all of the cells below it, apart from the ½ day courses.

8. Reposition the table so that it is in the centre of the pale blue area.

9. Save the publication as **Courses** and close it.

Exercise 50 - Merging and Splitting Cells

Guidelines:

Cells that are next to each other in a table can be merged to produce a larger cell. Once they have been merged, cells can be split to return to their original state. Cells that have not previously been merged cannot be split.

Actions:

1. You are the chef who runs the canteen for a local police station and have decided to keep a proper record of what is sold each day, because you keep running out of doughnuts. You intend to print out copies of a table to be completed each day. On a new publication, draw a large table in the centre of the page with **10** rows and **5** columns. Select the **Table format** option as **None** and click **OK**.

2. Use **Table | Select | Table** to select the whole table. Click the **Line/Border Style** button, ☰ and then select **More Lines**.

3. From the **Presets** area of the **Format Table** dialog box, select the **Grid** button, ⊞, then click **OK**. This ensures that all the cell borders are printed.

4. Select the second, third, fourth and fifth cells on the first row, by clicking and dragging across them, then select **Table | Merge Cells**.

5. With the merged cell selected, select **Table | Split Cells** to divide it into four separate cells again. **Undo** the last action.

6. Merge cells in the table and format it until it looks like the diagram opposite. The cells will need to be merged one row at a time.

7. Enter the text as opposite and format it as in the diagram.

8. Create a text box at the top of the page and enter your name.

9. Print one copy of the table.

10. Close the publication without saving.

Date	Department		
Product	Price	Quantity	Total Price
	Grand Total		

Exercise 51 - Creating Cell Diagonals

Guidelines:

Cells in a table can be split diagonally. This means that text can be entered in both parts of the same cell.

Actions:

1. On a new publication, draw a table with **3 rows**, **3 columns** and select **None** for the **Table format** option.

2. A table is to be created to record the scores of a battle re-enactment society, who each have their own battle site (playing field). In the first row and the first column, enter the data as in the table below, centring the text.

Battle Scores	Roundheads	Cavaliers
Roundheads	N/A	
Cavaliers		N/A

3. Enter **N/A** (not applicable), centred, in the cells as above, because the **Roundheads** could not fight themselves, etc.

4. Position the cursor in the third cell of the second row and select **Table | Cell Diagonals**. The **Cell Diagonals** dialog box appears.

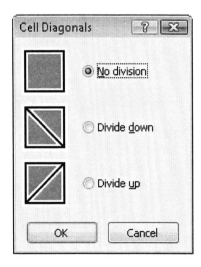

5. Select the **Divide up** option and click **OK**.

Exercise 51 - Continued

6. Position the cursor in the second cell of the third row and create another cell diagonal (**Divide up** again). The top half of these cells will show the home result and the bottom half will shows the away result.

7. Scores are for officers captured. Enter the scores as in the diagram below, pressing **<Tab>** or **<Shift Tab>** to move between cells. The **Cavaliers** won **3-2** away and lost **2-1** at home.

Battle Scores	Roundheads	Cavaliers
Roundheads	N/A	2-3 2-1
Cavaliers	1-2 3-2	N/A

8. For the scores, align the text in the top diagonals to the left and in the bottom to the right. Change the font of all text to **Blackadder ITC 16pt**. Resize the table if necessary.

9. To align the table text vertically, first select all text and then **Format | Table** and the **Cell Properties** tab. From **Vertical alignment** select **Middle** by clicking the drop down arrow.

10. Click **OK**.

11. To print all grid lines including diagonals, select **Table | Select | Table** and then right click on the table and select **Format Table**.

12. From the **Colors and Lines** tab, select the **Grid** option under **Presets**, then select the **Diagonal** option and set the **Line colour** to black. Click **OK** to apply the new settings.

Battle Scores	Roundheads	Cavaliers
Roundheads	N/A	2-3 2-1
Cavaliers	1-2 3-2	N/A

13. Print the publication and close it <u>without</u> saving.

Exercise 52 - Revision

1. Open the **Revision Project** publication (if the previous revision was not completed, open **Revision43** from the data files and save it immediately as **Revision Project**).

2. On the **Scratch Area**, create a table with **5** rows and **4** columns. If a message appears about the size of the table, click **Yes**.

3. Merge the cells on the top row and type in **Forthcoming Attractions**.

4. Widen columns **2** and **3**.

5. Enter text and format the table as below. The top row is filled with mid blue and the remaining rows are filled with a **20% tint** of the same blue. The font is **Garamond 11pt**, the top two rows are **Bold** and **Italic**.

Forthcoming Attractions			
Date	*Event*	*Location*	*Time*
Nov 29th	Christmas Lights	High Street	7 pm
Dec 13th	Santa's Parade	Starts Town Hall	4.30 pm
Dec 31st	New Year Celebrations	Leisure Centre	7.30 pm

6. Adjust the row height and column width to fit the text, as in the diagram.

7. Move the text box containing columns up and move the table on to the page, so the publication looks similar to the diagram below. If the items on your publication do <u>not</u> look like the diagram, resize or move all objects to match it.

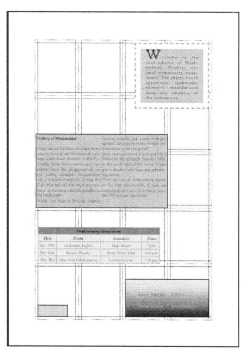

8. Save the changes to the publication and close it.

Section 6

Pictures

By the end of this Section you should be able to:

Use the Insert Clip Art Task Pane

Insert and Delete Pictures

Import Pictures

Move, Resize and Crop Pictures

Add Borders and Colour

Create Watermarks

Wrap Text around Pictures

Exercise 53 - The Insert Clip Art Task Pane

Guidelines:

Pictures can be added to a publication in two ways: either by importing a picture file, or by using the **Clip Gallery**. The **Clip Art** task pane contains graphics, which are sorted into categories, so the appropriate clip can be found quickly using a keyword search.

Actions:

1. On a new publication, click the **Picture Frame** button, and select **Clip Art**. The **Clip Art** task pane opens.

2. Click in the **Search for** box, delete any existing text and type in **animals**.

3. Click **Go**. After a short while, matching clips will be displayed - scroll down to see some of them.

4. To change the search, delete the **animals** search text and enter **people**. Click **Go**.

Exercise 53 - Continued

5. Click [Organize clips...] to display the **Organizer**.

Note: If an ***Add Clips to Organizer*** *dialog box appears, click* ***Later***.

6. Expand **Office Collections** by clicking the ⊞ at the left.

7. In the same way, expand the **Sports** collection and click **Athletes** to reveal the associated clips.

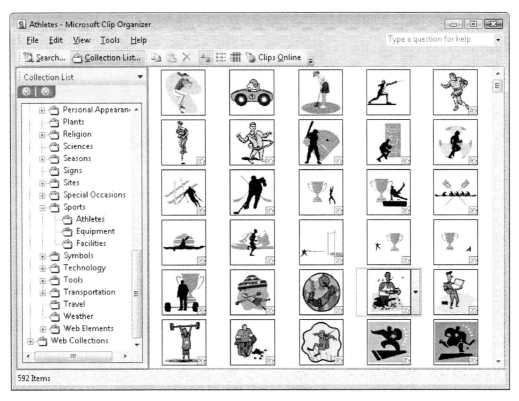

8. Look through some of the categories and then close the **Organizer**.

Exercise 54 - Inserting and Deleting Pictures

Guidelines:

There are various ways to insert a graphic from the **Clip Art** task pane, such as clicking on it, dragging it on to the page, or using the drop down menu that is provided for each graphic.

Actions:

1. Using the publication created in the previous exercise, search for clips of **people**.

2. Scroll to locate the following picture (use an alternative if it is unavailable):

3. Click on the picture and, holding down the mouse, drag it out of the task pane and on to the page. Click away from the picture to deselect it.

Note: A graphic can be inserted quickly by clicking on it.

4. Modify the search to look for clips of **weather** and scroll to locate the following clip:

Note: If you don't have an Internet connection you may have to select an alternative clip.

5. Move the mouse over the right of the picture and click the arrow. Select **Insert** from the menu to insert the picture.

*Note: A clip from the **Organizer** can be inserted by selecting it and clicking*
*   **Copy**, 🖼, *then in the publication, clicking **Paste**, 🖼.*

6. Select the **people** picture and press <**Delete**>. The picture disappears.

7. Close the **Clip Art** task pane and close the publication <u>without</u> saving.

Exercise 55 - Importing a Picture

Guidelines:

Another way to add a picture to a publication is to insert a picture file. The correct name for this is **importing**.

Actions:

1. Using a blank publication, click the **Picture Frame** button, and select **Picture from File**.

2. At the top left side of the page, click and drag to draw a picture frame. The **Insert Picture** dialog box is displayed.

3. Make sure the dialog box shows the location where the data files are saved and the **Files of type** box shows **All Pictures** (pictures can be saved in several different formats).

4. Click once on the file named **Ostrich**.

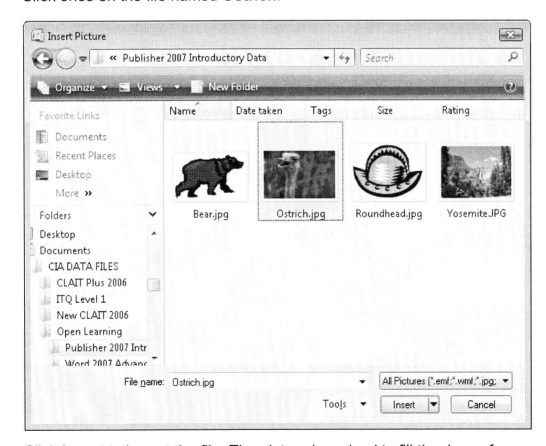

5. Click **Insert** to import the file. The picture is resized to fill the drawn frame, although the frame changes shape, if necessary, to maintain the proportions of the picture.

6. Leave the publication open for the next exercise.

Exercise 56 - Moving, Resizing & Cropping Pictures

Guidelines:

Pictures can be moved about the page and resized in the same way as any other object. Sometimes, only part of a picture might need to be included in a publication. If this is the case, the picture can be **cropped**.

Actions:

1. With the **Ostrich** picture selected, move it to the top left corner of the page by clicking anywhere on the picture (not a handle) and dragging it upward until it touches the top and left margins.

Note: *If necessary, refer back to Exercise 34, to refresh your memory about moving and resizing objects.*

2. Resize it to fill the top half of the page by dragging the bottom right handle down and to the right.

3. If the **Picture** toolbar is not displayed, select **View | Toolbars | Picture**. With the **Ostrich** picture still selected, click once on the **Crop Picture** button, ⌐┲, on the **Picture** toolbar.

4. Now move the mouse pointer over the middle handle at the right of the picture until the pointer changes to ⊦, ready to crop.

5. Click and drag to the left until most of the greenery is cropped, then release the mouse.

6. Crop the other edges of the picture in the same way until only the ostrich's head remains.

7. Click ⌐┲ again to deselect the cropping tool.

8. Click **Reset Picture**, ⌐▨, to return the picture to its original state (this will be its original state before it was resized to fit the frame).

9. Close the publication <u>without</u> saving the changes.

Exercise 57 - Adding Borders and Colour

Guidelines:

Borders and **Border Art** can be added to pictures in exactly the same way as to other objects. Background colour can also be added using the **Fill Color** techniques learned earlier. The same principles apply when working with any kind of object.

Actions:

1.   Open the publication **Battles**.

2.   At the bottom right of the page, draw a picture frame and import the file **Roundhead** from the data files.

3.   Add a **2pt** blue border.

4.   At the top left of the page, insert the following clip from the **Clip Art** task pane (search for **crown**):

Note: *If this clip is not available, use an alternative.*

5.   Apply a border to the picture, choosing any colour and style.

6.   Fill the frame with a colour of your choice.

7.   Save the publication as **Battles2**.

8.   Leave it open for the next exercise.

Exercise 58- Creating a Watermark Effect

Guidelines:

Colours and shades can be changed to allow pictures to be used in different ways. A frame can be masked, or partially covered, to apparently change its shape.

Actions:

1. Right click on the **Roundhead** picture to display the shortcut menu. Select **Format Picture** and click the **Recolor** button from the **Picture** tab. The **Recolor Picture** dialog box is displayed.

2. Drop down the **Color** list and select **Fill Effects**.

3. Only **Tint** is available. To create a watermark effect, change the **Base Color** to **Black** and select a **20%** tint:- the third box.

*Note: Watermarks can be created in different colours by selecting a different **Base Color**.*

4. Click **OK** three times to apply the effect.

5. The picture has changed to a pale grey, any original colours will be lost. Change the border to grey too.

6. Select the other graphic (the crown) and display the **Format Picture** dialog box.

7. Select the **Color** drop down arrow and select **Washout** from the list.

8. Click **OK**. The image now has a watermark effect but the original colours are still maintained (you may have to expand the image to see them).

9. Save the publication with the same name and close it.

Exercise 59 - Wrapping Text around Pictures

Guidelines:

When text and pictures are combined in the same publication, **Text Wrap** is used to decide how the text flows around the picture. Normally, the picture is contained within a rectangular picture frame and the text flows around this frame. However, this can be adjusted so the text wraps more closely to the picture.

Actions:

1. Open the publication **Tourist**. Increase the font size to **14** and increase the text box if necessary to fit in the text. Zoom in to **66%**.

2. Draw a picture frame in the middle of the first paragraph; this is to contain a picture from file.

3. Import the **Yosemite** picture.

4. The text flows around the picture, stopping at the picture frame. Move the picture upwards to see how the text re-aligns itself. Make the picture slightly bigger.

5. Increase the size of the text box if necessary.

6. Now import the **Bear** picture from the data files into the second paragraph and increase it to twice its original size.

7. With the picture selected, click the **Text Wrapping** button, .

8. Click the **Edit Wrap Points** button, . The picture now has a red border.

9. Zoom in to see the picture clearly.

10. Click at a point at the top of the red border and drag it up to change the way the text wraps around the picture.

11. Drag some of the other handles to change the style of the wrap.

12. Use the **Text Wrapping** button, , to change the wrap to **Tight** to see the changes.

    *Note: If a prompt about creating a new wrap boundary appears, click **No**.*

13. Add a text box at the bottom of the page and enter your name.

14. Print the publication and close it <u>without</u> saving.

Exercise 60 - Revision

1. Open the **Revision Project** publication (if the previous revision was not completed, open **Revision52** from the data files and save it immediately as **Revision Project**).

2. Search for a **Clip Art** graphic using the search **meadow**.

3. Select the following clip (or use an alternative clip, or an alternative search, e.g. **nature**):

4. Drag the picture to the **Scratch Area**. Resize it, using a corner handle, to around **3 x 4cm**.

5. Move the picture into the top right corner of the **History of Meadowdene** text box and wrap the text **Tight** to the picture (use [×]). If necessary, resize the text box to accommodate the text.

6. Delete the text box containing your name.

7. Move the **Contacts** text box on to the **Scratch Area** and move the table into the bottom left corner.

8. Now move **Contacts** directly beneath the **History of Meadowdene** text box.

9. Insert a second clip of your choice in the bottom right corner, using the search **people** or **playground**.

10. Resize the picture to fit. Resize the table if necessary.

11. Save the changes to the **Revision Project** publication and close it.

Note: See the Answers at the back of the guide for an idea of how your publication should look.

Section 7

WordArt

By the end of this Section you should be able to:

Create WordArt

Edit WordArt Text

Change WordArt Shape

Change Letter Height and Spacing

Rotate WordArt

Flip Text

Exercise 61 - WordArt

Guidelines:

WordArt, the feature that helps to create special text effects, is accessed using the **WordArt Tool**. A selection of **WordArt** styles is available, such as stretched text, curved text, etc. It is best to apply **WordArt** to small amounts of text only.

Actions:

1. On a blank publication, click **Insert WordArt**, 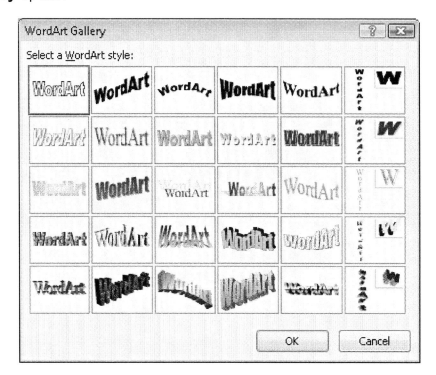 and the **WordArt Gallery** opens.

2. Select the fourth style from the third row and click **OK** to reveal the **Edit WordArt Text** dialog box.

3. Leave the box on screen for the next exercise.

Exercise 62 - Editing WordArt Text

Guidelines:

It is necessary to edit the **WordArt** text before it is inserted into a publication.

Actions:

1. The **Edit WordArt Text** dialog box is on the screen. Delete **Your Text Here** and type in your own name.

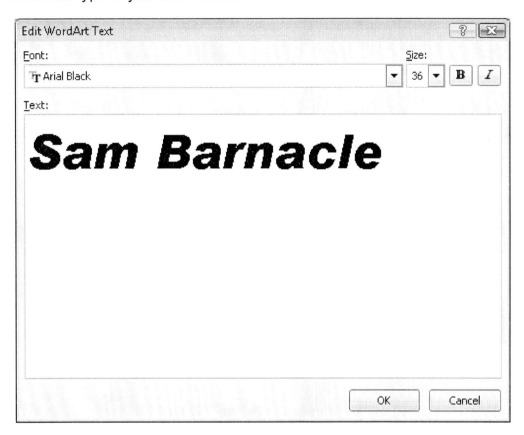

2. Click **OK** to add the **WordArt** to the page.

3. Move it into the centre if necessary and zoom in.

4. Click **Edit Text** on the **WordArt** toolbar.

5. To change the font, click the **Font** drop down list and select **Algerian**. Click **OK**.

6. Leave the publication open for the next exercise.

*Note: To edit the **WordArt** at any time in the future, double click on it.*

Exercise 63 - Changing WordArt Shape

Guidelines:

WordArt shape can be changed at any time.

Actions:

1. Using the publication from the previous exercise, select the WordArt.

2. Click the **WordArt Shape** button, 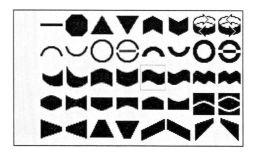 .

3. Try a few of the shapes to see how the **WordArt** changes.

4. Depending on the number of letters in your name, the styles will look different. Select the **Wave 1** style, ◤◢ .

5. With the **WordArt** selected, try clicking and dragging it by a yellow handle to see how the text is affected.

6. When you are happy with the **WordArt**, print the publication.

7. Close the publication <u>without</u> saving.

Exercise 64 - Changing Letter Height and Spacing

Guidelines:

It is possible to change the way **WordArt** looks by making all of the letters the same height, or changing the spacing between them. Sometimes, altering the character spacing can make the text easier to read.

Actions:

1. Open the publication **Best Friend** and click **Insert WordArt**, choosing the third style from the bottom row.

2. Enter **Labradors** in the **Edit WordArt Text** dialog box and click **OK**.

3. Move the **WordArt** to the **Scratch Area** and zoom in.

4. Change the font to **Lucida Bright**, make it **Bold** and click **OK**.

5. To make the characters the same height, click the **WordArt Same Letter Heights** button, [Aa]. The characters looked better originally. Click [Aa] again to remove the effect.

6. To change the character spacing, click [AV].

7. Select the **Loose** option.

8. The text would look more effective with tighter spacing. Adjust the **Spacing** to **Tight**. This makes the text easier to read.

9. Drag the **WordArt** on to the page, above the picture and the text box. Resize the **WordArt** to fill the white area at the top of the page.

10. Save the publication as **Best Friend2** and leave it open for the next exercise.

Exercise 65 - Rotating WordArt

Guidelines:

Rotating **WordArt** may make it a better fit for the publication.

Actions:

1.   Using the publication **Best Friend2**, make sure the **WordArt** is selected.

2.   Click and drag the green handle to the left to rotate it.

Note: *To rotate the **WordArt** by 15° intervals, hold down <**Shift**> while clicking and dragging.*

3.   Click on the text box to select it.

4.   Increase the size of the text box until it fits the white space at the bottom of the page. Increase the font size to **16pt**.

5.   Move and resize the **WordArt** until the publication looks similar to the diagram below.

6.   Increase the size of the picture slightly until the text fills the text box, then save the publication with the same name and close it.

Exercise 66 - Flip Text

Guidelines:

If **WordArt** has to fit a narrow space, at the side of a publication for example, without turning it on its side, the text can be flipped.

Actions:

1. Open the publication **Opening**. Insert **WordArt** using the fifth style on the second row of the **Gallery**.

2. Change the **WordArt** text to **One Night Only** and click **OK**. The text needs to fit the left side of the poster.

3. Click the **WordArt Vertical Text** button, . The text flips so it reads from top to bottom.

4. Change the font to **Engravers MT**. This changes the text to upper case.

5. Move the **WordArt** to the same position as in the diagram below, extending it top and bottom.

6. Draw a small text box at the bottom of the page and enter your name.

7. Print the publication, then close it <u>without</u> saving.

Exercise 67 - Revision

1.   Open the **Revision Project** publication (if the previous revision was not completed, open **Revision60** from the data files and save it immediately as **Revision Project**).

2.   Insert **WordArt**, choosing the fourth style from the fifth row of the gallery.

3.   Enter the text **Meadowdene Weekly**.

4.   Change the font to **Kristen ITC** and click **OK**.

5.   Move the **WordArt** to the top left of the page and resize it until it just overlaps the text box.

6.   Save the changes to the **Revision Project** publication and close it.

Note: See the Answers at the back of the guide for an idea of how your publication should look

Section 8

Working with Objects

By the end of this Section you should be able to:

Select Multiple Objects

Flip and Rotate Objects

Cut, Copy and Paste Objects and Text

Layer, Nudge and Align Objects

Use Drawing Objects

Exercise 68 - Selecting Multiple Objects

Guidelines:

Sometimes, it may be desirable to move, resize or rotate several objects at the same time. There are various ways of doing this. When the required objects have been selected, they can be grouped, so that they can be moved together, as a single object.

Actions:

1.   On a new publication, insert any **Clip Art** graphic at the top of the page, using the search **emotions**.

2.   Insert a second clip, this time using the search **entertainment**, at the bottom of the page.

3.   Click on the first clip to select it. Now click on the second clip and the first is deselected.

4.   To select both clips, click on the first clip, then press and hold down **<Shift>**.

5.   Click on the second clip whilst holding down **<Shift>**.

6.   Move the second clip to the right and the first clip is also moved.

7.   Notice the box that has appeared at the bottom of the selection, 🔲. This is called the **Group Objects Smart Tag** and indicates that the selected objects can be grouped.

8.   Insert a clip in the middle of the page, using the search **plants**.

9.   Use the mouse to click and drag a dotted line box around the three objects. They are all selected.

10. De-select the objects by clicking away from them.

11. Select **Edit | Select All** to select every object on the page.

12. Use the green handle to rotate one object. All objects are rotated.

13. Click **Group Objects**, 🔲. All the objects have now become one large object. Rotate it using the green handle and notice the difference to the previous step.

14. Click **Ungroup Objects**, 🔲. There are three separate objects again.

15. Close the publication <u>without</u> saving.

Exercise 69 - Flip and Rotate Objects

Guidelines:

When working with objects it is worth remembering that the same principles apply to different types of objects. Any object can be flipped to the left or the right by 90 degrees to create a different effect. An object can be rotated through <u>any</u> angle.

Actions:

1. Open the publication **Boulevard** and select the picture of the **Eiffel Tower**.

2. Select **Arrange | Rotate or Flip | Rotate Left 90°** to turn the picture on to its side.

3. Select the same command to turn the picture upside down.

4. Select **Arrange | Rotate or Flip | Flip Vertical** to flip the picture back to the correct way up, but a mirror position.

5. Select **Arrange | Rotate or Flip | Flip Horizontal** to flip the picture back to its original starting position.

6. Select all of the objects and rotate them 90 degrees to the left.

7. Undo the last action.

8. De-select the objects.

9. Use the green handle on the Eiffel Tower picture to rotate it to the right (hold down <**Shift**> while dragging).

10. Insert a suitable **Clip Art** graphic below **Visit the Landmarks of Paris**.

11. Resize the image appropriately.

12. Use its green handle to rotate it slightly to the left.

13. Draw a small text box at the bottom left of the page and enter your name.

14. Format this text box as desired.

15. Fill the large white text box with a **40% tint** of pale blue.

16. Print the publication.

Note: *See the Answers at the back of the guide for a sample of how your publication should look.*

17. Close the publication <u>without</u> saving.

Exercise 70 - Cut, Copy and Paste Objects

Guidelines:

The **Cut**, **Copy** and **Paste** commands are used to move objects from one place to another. Objects can be cut or copied within the same publication or from one publication and pasted into another. It is important to remember that if an object is cut, it is <u>removed</u> from its original position, but if it is copied, the original is <u>not</u> removed.

Actions:

1. On a new publication, insert the clip opposite (use an alternative if this clip is unavailable), using the search **cat**:

2. With the object selected, click the **Cut** button, ✂. The clip has been removed to the *Windows* **Clipboard**, a storage area which works behind the scenes, until it is pasted back into a publication.

Note: *The **Clipboard** can be viewed via the task pane - objects can be pasted by clicking their icon on the **Clipboard**.*

3. Click the **Paste** button, 📋. The clip reappears.

4. Click 📋 again to paste a second copy into the publication. It is pasted on top of the original. Move it away from the first image.

5. Insert the **Bear** picture from the data files into the publication.

6. Click the **Copy** button, 📋, then 📋 and a second picture is pasted on top of the first.

7. Move the second **Bear** picture to the bottom of the page and select **Edit | Copy**.

8. Open the publication **Tourist**. Select **Edit | Paste** to paste the picture into this publication. Click 📋 to add a second picture.

9. Move one to the top of the text box and the other to the bottom of the text box.

10. Leave **Tourist** open for the next exercise, but close the unsaved publication <u>without</u> saving.

Note: *If a message about saving the **Clipboard** appears, select **No**.*

Exercise 71 - Cut, Copy and Paste Text

Guidelines:

Text can be cut, copied and pasted in a similar way to objects, or it can be dragged from one place to another.

Actions:

1. Using the publication **Tourist**, select the text box and zoom in to read the text.

2. Select the first sentence and click .

3. Draw a text box at the bottom of the page and click .

4. The **Paste** smart tag, , appears. Click it to see pasting options.

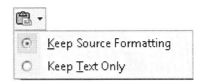

5. Click away from the displayed options to close them.

*Note: If a message appears about **AutoFlow**, click **No** and enlarge the text box.*

6. Change the font of the pasted text to **Georgia**, increase the size to **18pt** and make it bold.

7. Resize the text box if necessary.

8. Now move back to the top text box and select the first sentence, **Half Dome is a massive rock...**

9. Move the mouse over the selected text.

10. Click and drag the sentence to the end of the text. Adjust the spacing if necessary.

11. Select the word **Ahwahneechee** and hold down <**Ctrl**> while you drag it to the end of the text. When the mouse is released, the word is copied.

12. Close the publication without saving any changes.

Exercise 72 - Layering, Aligning & Nudging Objects

Guidelines:

To create a certain type of effect, objects can be moved about and placed on top of each other, so that some objects are partially covered. Some objects are at the bottom of the pile and others are at the top. Objects can be lined up automatically, either horizontally or vertically. To position objects more precisely, they can be nudged into position. The selected objects can be moved by a fraction, or by a more exact distance.

Actions:

1. Open the publication **Boulevard** and one at a time, move each object on top of the others in the following order: picture, **WordArt**, large text box, small text box. Some objects will not be visible at this stage.

2. Now shuffle the objects around to change their order. Select the **Visit the Landmarks of Paris** text box and click the drop down arrow on the **Send to Back** button, 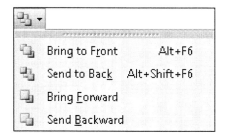, on the **Standard** toolbar.

Note: *The button changes to show the last positioning option chosen, so it may not be Send to Back but the menu options are the same.*

Bring to Front	Alt+F6
Send to Back	Alt+Shift+F6
Bring Forward	
Send Backward	

3. Select **Send to Back**. It may look as though the text box has disappeared, but it is behind the other objects, even the blue background frame.

4. Select **Arrange | Order | Bring Forward** to move the text box one place forward.

5. Repeat this action to move the text box forward again.

6. Now select the **Eiffel Tower** picture and click the **Bring to Front** button, , which will be displayed by clicking the drop down arrow.

7. With the picture still selected, select **Arrange | Order | Send Backward**.

Exercise 72 - Continued

8. Practise moving the objects backwards and forwards using the following options:

    Bring to Front   Places selected object on top of pile

    Send to Back   Places selected object at bottom of pile

    Bring Forward   Brings selected object forward one place

    Send Backward   Sends selected object back one place

9. Send the blue background to the back.

10. Now move all of the objects away from each other to any position on the page.

11. To line up all of the objects, first select them all (but not the large blue text box acting as a background).

12. Select **Arrange | Align or Distribute** and make sure **Relative to Margin Guides** is <u>not</u> selected. This means alignment will only be relative to the group of objects selected.

13. Select **Arrange | Align or Distribute | Align Center**. The centre of each object is now aligned.

14. Select **Arrange | Align or Distribute | Align Bottom**. The objects will now all overlap.

15. Move the objects away from each other.

16. Select the **WordArt** and the picture and align their right edges, using **Arrange | Align or Distribute | Align Right**.

17. Select the picture of the Eiffel Tower.

18. Select **Arrange | Nudge | Right** to move the picture slightly to the right.

19. Objects can be aligned relative to the blue margin guides around the page. In this publication, the blue background covers the margin guides. Select and delete the background text box.

20. Select **Arrange | Align or Distribute | Relative to Margin Guides**. Any further alignment will now be made relative to the page.

21. With all of the objects selected, select **Arrange | Align or Distribute | Align Middle**.

22. Notice that the objects are aligned to the middle of the top and bottom margin guides.

23. Close the publication <u>without</u> saving.

Exercise 73 - Drawing Objects

Guidelines:

Drawings can be created within *Publisher*. There are five drawing tools to assist with publications.

Actions:

1. Start a new publication. The **Drawing Tools** are at the left of the screen.

    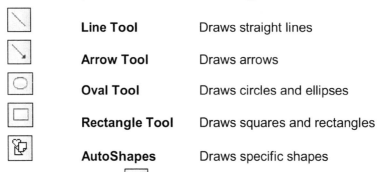

	Line Tool	Draws straight lines
	Arrow Tool	Draws arrows
	Oval Tool	Draws circles and ellipses
	Rectangle Tool	Draws squares and rectangles
	AutoShapes	Draws specific shapes

2. Select the **Arrow**, [arrow icon], then click and drag an arrow at the top of the page.

3. Click the **Arrow Style** button, [icon], on the **Formatting** toolbar and choose **Arrow Style 4** to make the arrow double headed.

4. With the arrow still selected, select the **Line/Border Style** button [icon] and then **More Lines** to change the arrowhead style (the **Dash Style** button, [icon], is also available for line/arrow formatting).

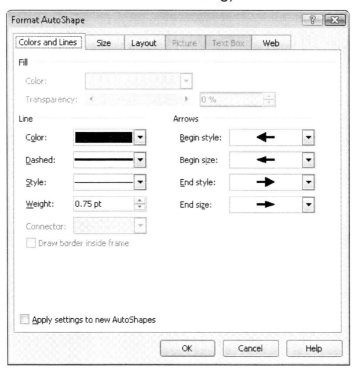

Exercise 73 - Continued

5.   In the **Weight** box change the point size to **12**.

6.   Drop down the **Line Color** list and select **orange**.

7.   Click **OK** to apply the changes.

8.   Select the **Rectangle Tool**, ▢. Hold down **<Shift>** while clicking and dragging on the page to create a perfect square.

9.   Use the **Oval Tool**, ⬭, to draw an ellipse underneath the square.

10. Now click the **AutoShapes** tool, ▧ and select **Basic Shapes**.

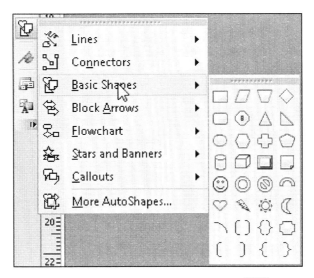

11. From the pop up menu, select the lightening bolt, ◿.

12. Click and drag on the page to draw this shape.

13. In the bottom right corner of the page, draw a rectangle and fill it with purple. To create a custom shadow effect, copy and paste the rectangle.

14. Fill the top rectangle with a paler shade of purple.

15. Now send the top rectangle to the back to finish creating the effect.

16. Colour the other shapes using the **Fill Color** button, ⬛▾. Add **Fill Effects** if desired.

17. Draw a small text box at the bottom of the page and enter your name.

18. Print the publication and close it <u>without</u> saving.

Exercise 74 - Revision

1.   Open the **Revision Project** publication (if the previous revision was not completed, open **Revision67** from the data files and save it immediately as **Revision Project**).

2.   Select the **WordArt** and hold down <Shift> while rotating it to the left by about **30º.**

3.   Reduce the size of the **WordArt** so that it fits between the top and left margins on the page.

4.   Draw a large text box that stretches from margin to margin, covering all objects on the page.

5.   Fill the text box with pale green and send it to the back.

6.   Select the **History of Meadowdene** text box and the picture around which its text is wrapped and group them.

7.   Nudge the grouped object to the right three times.

8.   Copy the picture at the bottom right of the page and paste it at the top left corner of the **History...** text box, but beneath the title.

9.   Reduce the size of the pasted picture only until all of the text can be seen and flip it horizontally.

10.   Move the picture in the bottom right corner up by about **2cm**.

11.   Move the table slightly to the right so that the top right corner of the table overlaps the lower left corner of the picture. Make sure the picture is behind the table.

12.   Draw a **AutoShape** from the **Stars and Banners** group on top of the **WordArt** and rotate it to the same angle as the **WordArt**.

13.   Move the shape on top of the **WordArt**, making sure it is slightly bigger.

Exercise 74 - Continued

14.   Fill the shape with purple and send it backward one level.

15.   Resize the **Custom Shape**, if necessary, so that the spikes can be seen around the edge of the **WordArt**.

16.   Apply the **Circles and Lines Border Art** to the large green text box, changing the **Weight** to **24pt**.

17.   Adjust the objects within the text box so that the **Border Art** can be seen properly.

18.   Using the techniques learned so far, make any changes you think will improve the appearance of the publication.

19.   Use the **Design Checker** and make amendments if you agree with them.

20.   Save the changes to the publication.

21.   Print the publication and then close it.

Note: *See the Answers at the back of the guide for an idea of how your finished publication should look.*

Section 9

Templates

By the end of this Section you should be able to:

Use Templates to Produce Various Publications

Create and Use a Template

Exercise 75 - Introduction to Templates

Guidelines:

Publisher's templates allow the creation of impressive one-page publications in a few steps.

Actions:

1. If the **Getting Started** window is not displayed then select **File | New** to display it.

2. In the **Getting Started** window, publications are grouped by publication type. Scroll down the list at the left and click on some of the different categories to watch the samples change.

3. Click on **Business Cards** and click on **Classic Designs** at the top of the window, then scroll down and select the **Eclipse** business card from the centre panel of the screen.

4. At the right of the window, under **Customize**, click the **Color scheme** drop down arrow and choose the **Aqua** colour scheme.

5. Select the **Deckle Font scheme** from the drop down list.

6. Click [Create] .

7. Delete the pyramid graphic on the business card.

8. Replace it with a clip of your choice.

9. Complete the information on the card with your own details.

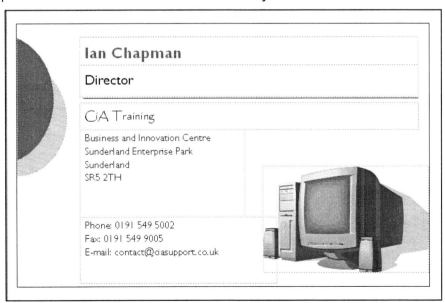

10. Save the publication as **Business Card** and close it.

Exercise 76 - Signs and Flyers

Guidelines:

Signs for work or home can easily be created using the task pane. If a special event is being arranged, why not use *Publisher* to create a flyer? A **Template** can help do this quickly.

Actions:

1. With the **Getting Started** window being viewed, select the **Signs** category from **Publication Types** and select the **Business Hours** sign.

2. Click the **Color scheme** drop down arrow at the right and choose **red**.

3. Change the **Font scheme** to **(default template fonts)** and click **Create**.

4. In the table, enter opening times of **09.00 to 17.30** for each day except Sunday, when the hours are **11.00 to 15.30**. Add an emergency phone number to the text box at the bottom of the page.

5. Print the publication and close it <u>without</u> saving.

6. From the **Getting Started** window, select **Flyers**, then scroll down the window to display the sub category **Event**.

7. Select the **Floating Oval Event Flyer** and choose the **Fjord Color scheme**.

8. Leave the remaining options as they stand, then click **Create**.

9. Change the **Event Title** to **Publishing Forum**, make the text bold and replace the bulleted list with the following **Highlights**:

    -   **Desktop Publishing Seminar**

    -   **Demonstration**

    -   **Workshop**

10. All techniques learned so far for manipulating objects apply to publications created using a templates. Make personal changes to the publication.

11. When satisfied with the result, print a copy of your flyer.

12. Close the publication <u>without</u> saving.

Exercise 77 - Certificates

Guidelines:

Award and gift certificates can be produced using the task pane. Use the techniques learned so far to add a personal touch.

Actions:

1. From the **Getting Started** window, select the **Award Certificates** category.

2. From the options, choose the certificate of **Achievement**.

3. Select the **Waterfall Color scheme**.

4. Click **Create**.

5. Do not change the **Certificate of Achievement** text box, but change the font of the others to **Bradley Hand ITC**.

6. Replace **Name of Recipient** with your own name.

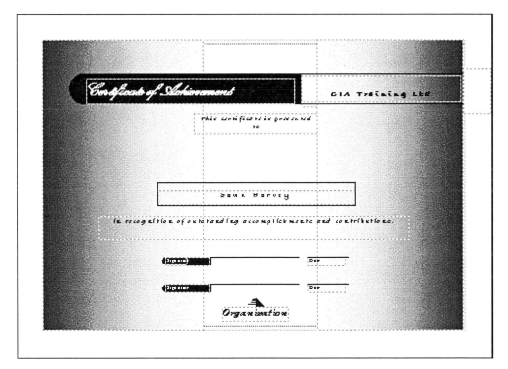

7. In the text box below your name, replace the text with **In recognition of the successful completion of the Introductory Open Learning Guide for Publisher 2007**.

8. Print the certificate, then close the publication <u>without</u> saving.

Exercise 78 - Greeting Cards

Guidelines:

Publisher has lots of samples to help you design greeting cards for different occasions.

Actions:

1. From the **Getting Started** window, **Publications Types**, select the **Greeting Cards** category and the **Birthday** sub category.

2. Select **Birthday 12**.

3. From the **Layout Options** at the right of the screen, select **Greetings Bar**.

4. Make sure **Quarter page side fold** is selected from **Page size** options.

5. Choose the **Orchid Color scheme** then click **Create**.

6. Click **Select a suggested verse** from the task pane. Choose any of the available options and click **OK**.

7. Close the task pane.

8. Notice how the number of pages in the publication are displayed on the **Status Bar** (multiple page publications will be covered in the Advanced Guide).

Exercise 78 - Continued

9.   Click on page 2 to display the inside of the card - pages 2 and 3.

10. Double click on the picture on page 2 and replace it with an alternative of your choice using the **Clip Art** task pane.

11. Close the task pane and fill the text boxes on page 3 with a **Gradient** fill effect using blue and yellow.

12. Move to page 4 and make sure the lower text box shows your name.

13. Save the publication as **Birthday**.

14. Print the card and fold it.

15. Close the publication.

Exercise 79 - CD/DVD Labels

Guidelines:

Labels for CDs or DVDs can be created from a wizard and printed on special CD label paper. It is also possible to create paper inserts that fit into jewel cases, where the contents of the disk and any additional information can be listed.

Actions:

1. From the **Getting Started** window, select the **Labels** category and then select **CD/DVD labels**.

2. Select the circular **Mosaic** design and click **Create**. Leave the task pane displayed on the left.

3. Look at the **Label Options** section of the task pane to see the size of label required for this publication.

4. Change the **Color Scheme** to **Aqua**.

5. Replace the egg timer graphic with a **Clip Art** graphic of your choice.

6. Print the publication and then close it <u>without</u> saving.

7. Start a new publication and select the **CD/DVD Labels** category again.

8. This time select the **Mosaic design** for CD case insert, a matching design found to the right of the previous selection.

9. Zoom in and read the suggested information for each area of the insert.

10. Notice again that the required size is displayed in the task pane.

11. Close the publication <u>without</u> saving.

Exercise 80 - Create a Template

Guidelines:

Any publication can be set up to be used as a template, i.e. a base from which other publications can be generated. *Publisher* has many templates already provided, you have already come across them while using the **Getting Started** window. A template can have text or pictures already added so that if several people needed to use the same template, then you can be sure that they are starting from the same point.

Once a template is saved, it can be used at any time to produce a publication. Templates are saved in a special place where they can all be kept together and used by everyone. They can, of course, be saved to any drive or disk, but would then not be available for general use.

Actions:

1. You are going to produce a template for a college newsletter. On a blank publication, draw a text box that fills the page and extends to all the margins.

2. Fill it with a **10% tint** of blue.

3. Insert **WordArt**, the 4th style on the 3rd row, and enter the text **Campus News**.

4. Move the **WordArt** to the top of the page, positioning it at the centre.

5. At the bottom of the page, draw another text box, between the margins, this time about **1.5cm** high.

6. Enter the text **Published by** and press <**Enter**>.

7. On the second line of the box enter the text **Date of Publication**. Format the text in this box as **Comic Sans MS 11pt**.

8. Place a **1pt** pale blue border around the box.

9. Zoom out so that you can see the whole page. Draw another text box that neatly fits between the **WordArt** and the lowest text box.

10. Format this box so that it has 2 columns.

11. With the text box still selected, fully justify the text (even though there isn't any yet).

12. Insert a suitable **Clip Art** graphic so that it overlaps both columns.

13. Resize the graphic to approximately **5½ x 4cm** and move it to the top centre of the text box.

Exercise 80 - Continued

14. Place a **1pt** green border around the picture. This forms the basis of the template and should look similar to the diagram below.

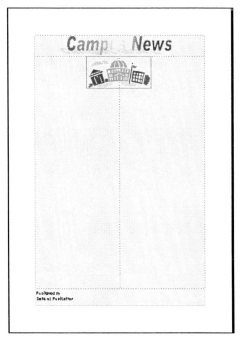

15. The template is now ready for all the week's news to be entered once it has been saved. Select **File | Save As**. At the dialog box, drop down the **Save as type** list and select **Publisher Template**.

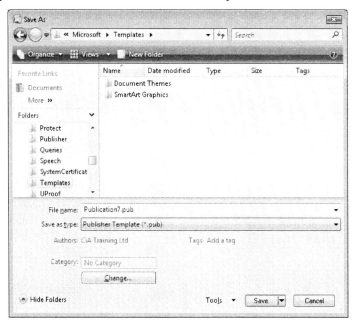

16. Notice how the **Save in** location has automatically changed to **Templates**. This is the place that all templates are stored by default.

17. In the **File name** box enter **Newsletter** and click **Save**. The template is now saved for repeated use.

18. Close the publication.

Exercise 81 - Use a Created Template

Guidelines:

Once a template has been created it can be accessed at any time and resaved just like any other publication.

When templates are no longer required they can be deleted from the list.

Actions:

1. From the **Getting Started** window, select **My Templates**.

2. The newly created **Newsletter** template will be shown, along with any other templates that may be available.

3. Select the **Newsletter** template and click **Create**.

4. The design you just created is now on screen. Insert the text file **Campus** from the data files into the text box with columns.

5. Increase the font of the imported text to **16pt**, adjusting the spacing and formatting as necessary so the text fits the box.

*Note: Depending on the **Clip Art** image selected, it may have to be reformatted and brought forward one level so that the text flows around it.*

6. In the lower box, insert your name after **Published by** and today's date after **Date of Publication**.

7. Save the publication by navigating to the data file location and naming the publication **Campus2**.

8. Print a copy of the publication.

9. Close the publication.

Note: Check the sample publication in Answers at the end of the guide.

10. To delete this template, display the **Getting Started** window.

11. Select **My Templates** from the list at the left.

12. Select the template **Newsletter** and click on the arrow at the right.

Exercise 81 - Continued

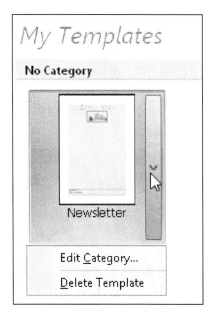

13.   Select **Delete Template**.

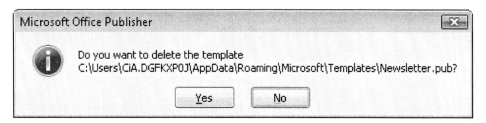

14.   At the dialog box select **Yes**.

Note: *To delete a template when Publisher is not open, display the **Computer** window. Display the template location (Local Disk (C:)\ User name\App Data\Roaming\Microsoft\Templates).*

          *If you cannot see any elements of this path, they may be hidden. Click the **Start** button on the **Taskbar** and then open the **Computer** window. Click **Organize** and select **Folder options** and the **View** tab. Make sure the **Show hidden files and folders option** is checked. Close the **Computer** window.*

Exercise 82 - Revision

1. Use the **Getting Started** screen to select a **Menu** publication, based on the **Daily Special** layout, using the **Scallops** design.

2. Use the **Peach Color scheme**.

3. Select the **Full-page** option from **Page size Options** at the right of the **Getting Started** window.

4. Complete the text boxes with appropriate items and change the font to **French Script MT**.

5. Increase the font size and character spacing as necessary to improve the menu's legibility.

6. Delete the **Organization** object at the bottom of the page (ensure both parts are deleted) and replace it with a suitable **Clip Art** graphic.

7. Rotate the picture **30°** to the right.

8. Save the publication as **Specials** and print it.

9. Close the publication.

Note: *The templates used in this Section are just a tiny selection of those available, why not try some more?*

10. Close *Publisher*.

Answers

Exercise 21

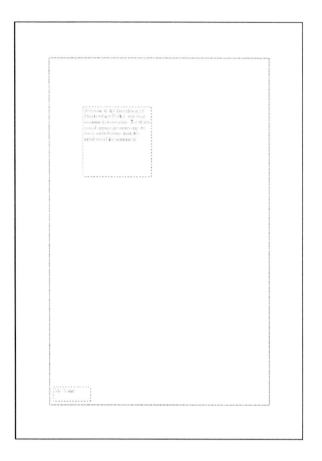

Exercise 24

abrador Retrievers are probably the most popular dogs in Britain and have a well-deserved reputation for their placid temperament. *Labradors can be black, yellow or chocolate and there are two strains of the breed: the show dog and the working dog.* The working dog, bred specifically for retrieving game, tends to be slimmer and more energetic than the larger show dog. **If you look carefully between a Labrador's toes, you will see that they are partially webbed.** *This is to help them swim – any Labrador owner will tell you that their dog adores the water. The dog's coat is very dense and waxy near the skin – once again, this is for waterproofing. Labradors, in common with other gundogs, have a rubbery kind of flap in their mouth, which goes over the teeth to protect the game they are retrieving. The Labrador is a very loyal animal who would, I am convinced, protect its owner with its life.*

Exercise 32

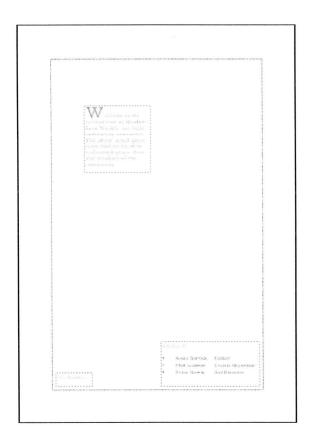

Exercise 43

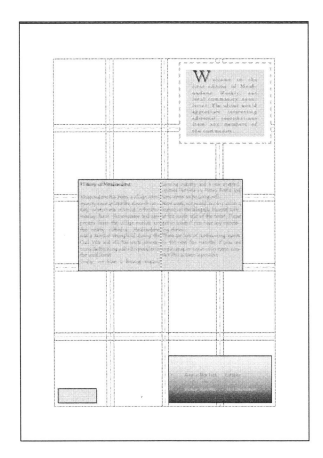

Exercise 60

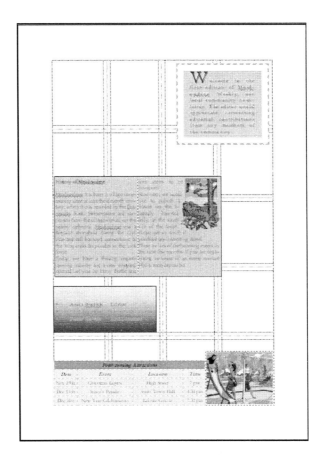

Exercise 67

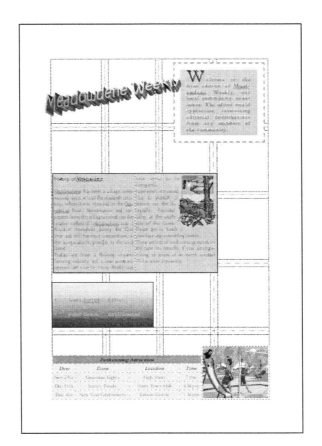

Exercise 69

Exercise 74

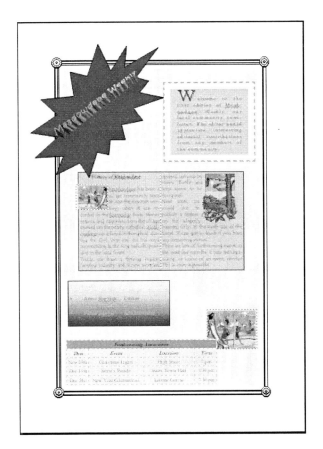

Exercise 81

Camp News

Freshers' Week

New students will be welcomed next week with various events for Freshers' Week. There will be introductions to the various clubs and societies that exist for college students, during informal talks in the Drama Theatre on Monday afternoon. On Wednesday there will be a tour of the campus for those who haven't already found their way around. Come to the Refectory on Thursday lunchtime to take part in a pie eating contest (see Charlie Bunter for details). Friday evening sees a sponsored pub crawl round the popular local watering holes. For more information on any of these events, contact Ranjit Patel, ext 2014.

College to Receive Funding for IT Suite

The college has secured full funding for a state of the art IT suite at the Midgely Road campus. 30 brand new PCs with 17" flat screen monitors and CD/DVD drives are to be supplied for the new term.

New Staff

The College would like to welcome the following new staff: Bill Wheatley – History, Sammy Lee – Asian Studies and Pru Quicksilver - Maths.

Car Parking

Would students please park in the designated bays only. There were four complaints last week that disabled spaces had been taken by non-permit holders.

Drama Season

The extremely popular drama season is to start again on 25th of this month, with a performance of The Crucible by Arthur Miller. Abigail is to be played by Katrina Popodopolos. Tickets are on sale now from the English Department or the Media Studies Department, priced at £2.50 each. All proceeds go to our Cancer Research appeal.

Published by My Name
Date of Publication 15th October 2007

Glossary

AutoShape	Pre-prepared shapes available within *Publisher*.
Crop	To remove unwanted areas of a picture.
Fill Effects	Coloured effects that can be used as a background for a text box or image.
Font	A type or style of print.
Group	To combine several selected objects into one.
Handles	The white circles that are displayed at the corners and at the centre of the sides of an object when it is selected.
Import	To insert text or pictures, which already exist in another location, into a publication.
Indent	An amount by which text is moved towards the vertical centre line of a page, away from a margin.
Justified	An alignment setting which straightens both the left and right margins of the text.
Kerning	An adjustment to the space between a pair of characters.
Layout	The arrangement of a publication to suit various purposes; **Special Fold** card, **Label**, **Envelope**, etc.
Layout Guides	Blue dotted lines around the page, which can help to line up objects on the page.
Margin Guides	Indicate the boundaries of the printed page.
Object	An item within a publication such as a picture, or a text box.
Objects Toolbar	A toolbar, that by default is positioned down the left side of the screen, enabling the creation of various objects on the page.
Orientation	Whether the page is arranged on its side or upright.
Page Setup	A facility that allows the layout and orientation of a publication to be specified.
Picture Frame	A frame that restricts the area in which a graphic image can be positioned and/or viewed.
Point	A unit of measurement of font size. 1 point equals 1/72 inch.

Publication	The universal name for a finished file created within *Publisher*.
Sans Serif	A style of font that does not have any decorative lines or curls on the "stalks" of letters.
Scaling	An adjustment to the width of characters.
Scratch Area	The grey area around the page that can be used to store text and pictures while the page layout is finalised.
Select	To highlight a section of text or click on an object to identify it for editing or formatting.
Serif	A style of font that has decorative lines or curls on the "stalks" of letters.
Taskbar	By default, a grey band across the bottom of the **Desktop**, which displays a button for each program that is currently running.
Template	A ready-made publication that requires only the text to be edited or a picture to be changed.
Text Box	An object into which text may be typed or imported.
Text Wrapping	The way text "flows" around a picture or other object positioned inside a text frame.
Tracking	An adjustment to the spacing between characters.
Zoom	A function that allows the degree of magnification of a page to be adjusted to suit the user.

Index

Alignment

Text 40

Object 100

Borders 55

Border Art 56

Picture 83

Bullets 45

Callouts 62

Certificates 109

Clip Gallery 78

Colour

Fill 57

Pictures 83

Text 38

Columns 61

In Tables 71, 72

Connecting Text Boxes 60

Cropping Pictures 82

Cursor Movement 25

Cut, Copy and Paste

Objects 98

Text 99

Design Checker 29

Drawing Objects 102

Drop Caps 36

Editing Text 27

Filling Text Boxes 57

Flip

Objects 97

Flyers 108

Format Painter 39

Greeting Cards 110

Grouping Objects 96

Help 13

Layering 100

Margins & Layout Guides 53

Menus 11

Nudging Objects 100

Numbering 45

Objects

Aligning 100

Cut, Copy and Paste 98

Drawing 102

Flip 97

Grouping 96

Layering 100

Nudging 100

Rotate 97

Selecting 96

Page Setup 30

Pictures

Borders 83

Clip Gallery 78

Colour 83

Cropping 82

Deleting 80

Importing 81

Inserting 80

Moving 82

Resizing 82

Watermark 84

Wrapping Text 85

Positioning and Sizing 16

Printing

Page Setup 30

Print Options 31

Print Options 31

Publications 19

Blank 9

Closing 22

Opening 23

Saving 20

Publisher

Closing 17

Screen 10

Starting 8

Redo 28

Resize Objects 52

Revision

Fundamentals 18

Objects 104

Pictures 86

Publications 32

Tables 76

Text Boxes 65

Text Formatting 49

Wizards 117

WordArt 94

Rotate

Objects 97

WordArt 92

Scratch Area 64

Selecting Text 26

Shadow 55

Sidebars 62

Signs 108

Sizing 16

Spacing

Character 41

Line 41

Paragraph 41

Spell Checking 47

Tables

Cell Diagonals 74

Change Column Width 71

Change Row Height 71

Deleting 70

Entering Text 68

Formatting Cells 69

Inserting 67

Inserting Rows/Columns 72

Merging Cells 73

Splitting Cells 73

Tabs 43

Task Pane 11

Templates

Certificates 109

Create 113

Delete 116

Flyers and Signs 108

Greeting Cards 110

Use 115

Text Boxes 14

Borders and Shadow 55

Columns 61

Connecting 60

Cursor Movement 25

Editing Text 27

Filling 57

Importing Text Files 59

Layout Guides 53

Margins 53

Moving 52

Resizing 52

Properties 51

Selecting Text 26

Spell Checking 47

Thesaurus 47

Text Files

Importing 59

Text Formatting

Bullets 45

Colour 38

Cut, Copy and Paste 99

Drop Caps 36

Effects 35

Fonts 34

Format Painter 39

Numbering 45

Size 34

Spacing 41

Tabs 43

Wrapping around Pictures 85

Thesaurus 47

Toolbars 11

Undo 28

Watermark 84

Wizards

WordArt 88

Changing Letter Height/Spacing 91

Changing Shape 90

Editing Text 89

Flip Text 93

Rotating 92

Zoom 15

Other Products from CiA Training

CiA Training is a leading publishing company, which has consistently delivered the highest quality products since 1985. A wide range of flexible and easy to use self teach resources has been developed by CiA's experienced publishing team to aid the learning process. These include the following materials at the time of publication of this product:

- **Open Learning Guides**

- **ECDL/ICDL & ECDL/ICDL Advanced (ECDL Foundation Qualification)**

- **New CLAIT, CLAIT Plus & CLAIT Advanced (OCR Qualification)**

- **CiA Revision Series**

- **ITQs (Industry Standard Qualification)**

- **e-Citizen (ECDL Foundation Qualification)**

- **Trainer's Packs with iCourse**

- **Start IT (City & Guilds Qualification)**

- **Skill for Life in ICT (Industry Standard Qualification)**

- **iCourse - Course customising software**

We hope you have enjoyed using our materials and would love to hear your opinions about them. If you'd like to give us some feedback, please go to:

www.ciatraining.co.uk/feedback.php

and let us know what you think.

New products are constantly being developed. For up to the minute information on our products, to view our full range, to find out more, or to be added to our mailing list, visit:

www.ciatraining.co.uk

Notes